Praying with
Padre Pio

Eileen Dunn Bertanzetti

the WORD
among us®
Press

The Word Among Us Press
9639 Doctor Perry Road, Ijamsville, Maryland 21754
www.wordamongus.org
ISBN: 978-1-59325-091-1
14 13 12 11 10   3 4 5 6 7

Cover Design: The DesignWorks Group
Cover photo: Stigmatic, by Keystone/Getty Images
Book Design: David Crosson

Made and printed in the United States of America.

Library of Congress Cataloging-in-Publication Data

Bertanzetti, Eileen Dunn.
    Praying with Padre Pio / Eileen Dunn Bertanzetti.
        p. cm.
    Includes bibliographical references.
    ISBN 978-1-59325-091-1 (alk. paper)
    1. Spiritual life—Catholic Church. 2. Catholic Church—Prayers and
devotions. 3. Pio, of Pietrelcina, Saint, 1887-1968. I. Title.
    BX2350.3.B475 2007
    242--dc22
                    2007015541

Contents

Foreword

Just as food is required for human life, so are companions. Indeed, the word "companions" comes from two Latin words: *com,* meaning "with," and *panis,* meaning "bread." Companions nourish our heart, mind, soul, and body. They are also the people with whom we can celebrate the sharing of bread.

Perhaps the most touching stories in the Bible are about companionship: the Last Supper, the wedding feast at Cana, the sharing of the loaves and the fishes, and Jesus' breaking bread with the disciples on the road to Emmaus. Each incident of companionship with Jesus revealed more about his mercy, love, wisdom, suffering, and hope. When Jesus went to pray in the Garden of Olives, he craved the companionship of the apostles. They let him down. But God sent the Spirit to inflame the hearts of the apostles, and they became faithful companions to Jesus and to each other.

Throughout history, other faithful companions have followed Jesus and the apostles. These saints and mystics have also taken the journey from conversion, through suffering, to resurrection. Just as they were inspired by the holy people who went before them, so too may you take them as your companions as you walk on your spiritual journey.

The Companions for the Journey series is a response to the spiritual hunger of Christians. This series makes available the rich spiritual teachings of mystics and guides whose wisdom can help us on our pilgrimage. Our hope is that, as you complete each meditation, you will feel supported, challenged, and affirmed by a soul-companion on your spiritual journey.

The spiritual hunger that has emerged in the last few decades is a great sign of renewal in Christian life. People fill retreat programs and workshops on topics in spirituality. The demand for spiritual directors exceeds the number available. Interest in the lives and writings of saints and mystics is increasing as people search for models of whole and holy Christian life.

PRAYING WITH THE SAINTS

Praying with Padre Pio is more than just a book about Pio's spirituality. This book seeks to engage you in praying in the way that Padre Pio did about issues and themes that were central to his experience. Each meditation can enlighten your understanding of his revelations and lead you to reflect on your own experience.

The goal of *Praying with Padre Pio* is that you will discover his wonderfully alive spirituality and integrate his spirit and wisdom into your relationship with God, with your brothers and sisters, and with your own heart and mind.

Suggestions for Praying with Padre Pio

Meet Padre Pio, a caring companion for your pilgrimage, by reading the Introduction, which begins on page 13. It provides a brief biography and the major themes of his spirituality.

Once you meet Padre Pio, you will be ready to pray with him and to encounter God, your human sisters and brothers, and yourself in new and wonderful ways. To help your prayer, here are some suggestions that have been part of the tradition of Christian spirituality:

Create a sacred space. Jesus said, "Whenever you pray, go into your room and shut the door and pray to your Father who is in secret; and your Father who sees in secret will reward you" (Matthew 6:6). Solitary prayer is best done in a place where you can have privacy and silence, both of which can be luxuries in the lives of busy people. If privacy and silence are not possible, create a quiet, safe place within yourself, perhaps while riding to and from work, while waiting in the dentist's office, or while waiting for someone. Do the best you can, knowing that a loving God is present everywhere. Whether the meditations in this book are used for solitary prayer or with a group, try to create a prayerful mood with candles, meditative music, a crucifix, or an image of Mary.

Open yourself to the power of prayer. Every human experience has a religious dimension. All of life is suffused with God's presence. So remind yourself that God is present as you begin your period of prayer. Do not worry about distractions. If something keeps intruding during your prayer, spend some time talking with God about it. Be flexible, because God's Spirit blows where it will.

Prayer can open your mind and widen your vision. Be open to new ways of seeing God, people, and yourself. As you open yourself to the Spirit of God, different emotions are evoked, such as sadness from tender memories, or joy from a celebration recalled. Our emotions are messages from God that can tell us much about our spiritual quest. Also, prayer strengthens our will to act. Through prayer, God can touch our will and empower us to live according to what we know is true.

Finally, many of the meditations in this book will call you to employ your memories, your imagination, and the circumstances of your life as subjects for prayer. The great mystics and saints realized that they had to use all of their resources to know God better. Indeed, God speaks to us continually and touches us constantly. We must learn to listen and feel with all the means that God gave us.

Come to prayer with an open mind, heart, and will.

Preview each meditation before beginning. Spend a few moments previewing the readings and especially the reflection activities. Several reflection activities are given in each meditation, because different styles of prayer appeal to different personalities or personal needs. *Note that each meditation has more reflection activities than can be done during one prayer period. Therefore, select only one or two reflection activities each time you use a meditation. Do not feel compelled to complete all of the reflection activities.*

Read meditatively. After you have placed yourself in God's presence, the meditations offer you a story about Pio and a selection from his writings. Take your time reading. If a particular phrase touches you, stay with it. Relish its feelings, meanings, and concerns.

Use the reflections. Following "Pio's Words" is a short reflection in commentary form, meant to give perspective to the readings. Then you will be offered several ways of meditating on the readings and the theme of the prayer. You may be familiar with the different methods of meditating, but in case you are not, they are described briefly here:

Repeated centering prayer. One means of focusing your prayer is to use a centering prayer. The prayer may be a single word or a short phrase taken from the readings or from the Scriptures. For example, a centering prayer for a meditation on courage might be "I go before you" or "trust." Repeated slowly in harmony with your breathing, the prayer helps you center your heart and mind on one action or attribute of God.

✿ *Lectio divina:* This type of meditation is "divine studying," a concentrated reflection on the word of God or the wisdom of a spiritual writer. Most often in *lectio divina*, you will be invited to read one of the passages several times and then concentrate on one or two sentences, pondering their meaning for you and their effect on you. *Lectio divina* commonly ends with formulation of a resolution.

✿ Guided meditation: In this type of meditation, our imagination helps us consider alternative actions and likely consequences. Our imagination helps us experience new ways of seeing God, our neighbors, ourselves, and nature. When Jesus told his followers parables and stories, he engaged their imagination. In this book you will be asked to follow a guided meditation.

One way of doing a guided meditation is to read the scene or story several times until you know the outline and can recall it when you enter into reflection. Or, before your prayer time, you may wish to record the meditation on a tape recorder. If so, remember to allow pauses for reflection between phrases and to speak with a slow, peaceful pace and tone. Then, during prayer, when you have finished the readings and the reflection commentary, you can turn on your recording of the meditation and be led through it. If you find your own voice too distracting, ask a friend to make the tape for you.

❧ Examen of consciousness: The reflections often will ask you to examine how God has been speaking to you in your past and present experience—in other words, the reflections will ask you to examine your awareness of God's presence in your life.

❧ Journal writing: Writing is a process of discovery. If you write for any length of time, stating honestly what is on your mind and in your heart, you will unearth much about who you are, how you stand with your God, what deep longings reside in your soul, and more. In some of the reflections, you may be asked to write a dialogue with Jesus or someone else. If you have never used writing as a means of meditation, try it. Reserve a special notebook for your journal writing. If desired, you can go back to your entries at a future time for an examen of consciousness.

❧ Action: Occasionally, a reflection may suggest singing a favorite hymn, going out for a walk, or undertaking some other physical activity. Actions can be meaningful forms of prayer.

Using the Meditations for Group or Family Prayer

If you wish to use the meditations for community prayer, these suggestions may be of help:

✿ Read the theme to the group. Call the group into the presence of God, using the short opening prayer. Invite one or two participants to read one or both of the readings. If you use both readings, observe the pause between them.

✿ You may decide to use the reflection as a reading or to skip it, depending on the needs and interests of the group.

✿ Select one of the reflection activities for your group. Allow sufficient time for your group to reflect, to do a centering prayer, to accomplish a studying prayer (*lectio divina*), or to finish an examen of consciousness. Depending on the group and the amount of time available, you may want to invite the participants to share their reflections, responses, or petitions with the group.

✿ Reading the passage from the Scriptures may serve as a summary of the meditation.

✿ If a formulated prayer or a psalm is given as a closing, it may be recited by the entire group. Or you may ask participants to offer their own prayers for the closing.

Now you are ready to pray with Padre Pio, a compassionate and challenging companion on your spiritual journey. May you find him to be a true companion for your soul.

Introduction

In September 1968, the Italian Capuchin priest known worldwide as Padre Pio felt extremely ill and weak. On September 22, he celebrated his usual 5:00 a.m. Mass, but felt so weak that he collapsed. At 2:30 the next morning, he passed away peacefully. His death made headlines all over the world.

During Padre Pio's eighty-one years, hundreds of thousands of pilgrims traveled to this humble man's monastery in San Giovanni Rotondo, Italy, to see and hear him, to confess to him, and to attend the Masses he celebrated. Pilgrims today still flock to San Giovanni and to Pio's crypt. Many thousands still ask Pio to intercede for them. While Pio lived, pilgrims from around the world often heard him say, "I can do even more for you after death." In fact, the church approved two miracles wrought through Padre Pio's intercession after his death, allowing Pope John Paul II to canonize him in 2002, proclaiming him "Saint" Padre Pio.

"Throughout the centuries, God has chosen some souls in whom he has renewed the passion of his Son in a very special manner," one biographer has observed, adding, "In the twentieth century, he chose Padre Pio."[1] Just like his Franciscan predecessor, St. Francis of Assisi, Padre Pio bore the stigmata—the bleeding wounds of Christ in his hands, feet, and side. In doing so, he reminded believers everywhere of the mystery, joy, and suffering to be found in the cross of Christ.

PIO'S STORY

In 1887, while the Industrial Revolution continued to help raise northern Italy's standard of living, southern Italy remained almost entirely preindustrial and poor. On May 25 of that same year, Francesco Forgione was born in Pietrelcina, a small village in southern Italy, to simple, devout, hardworking farmers, Orazio and Giuseppa Forgione.

In Pietrelcina as well as in all of southern Italy, the infant mortality rate was high. Nevertheless, even though two of the Forgione babies had died in infancy, five children, including Francesco, survived.

By the time he was five, Francesco had promised fidelity to St. Francis of Assisi. In spite of his poor health, young Francesco tried to imitate Francis by doing penance. For example, even though his mother provided him with a warm, soft bed, Francesco often slept on the cold stone floor. His parents taught their children to place God above all else, and Francesco did. His staunch faith and obedience to his parents set a strong example for his siblings and peers.

When he was old enough, Francesco often helped his parents tend their crops in the rocky fields. As the boy grew older, his father asked him what he wanted to do with his life. Francesco, who had seen the Franciscan Capuchin friars in their brown robes and beards, replied, "I want to be a monk with a beard."[2]

Francesco also wanted to enter the priesthood, but that would require many years of expensive schooling, which Orazio Forgione could not afford. Nevertheless, Orazio found a solution. Like hundreds of men in southern Italy, Orazio emigrated to America. There he toiled at common-labor jobs, each week sending nine American dollars to his wife, Giuseppa. With that small sum, she fed and clothed her five children and sent Francesco to school.

Francesco wanted to embrace the prayerful, austere life of the Capuchins, but he would have to leave his beloved family. In January 1903, fifteen-year-old Francesco courageously left home to enter the Capuchin Friary of Morcone. He donned the novice habit, and took the name Fra (Brother) Pio. By 1910, despite his perennially poor health, Pio completed the required studies. On August 10 he was ordained a priest.

Sickness and the Army

The day after his ordination, Padre (Father) Pio journeyed to Pietrelcina to celebrate his first Mass. Pio's family and friends attended, without Orazio, who still worked in America.

World War I and its horrors arrived, and in 1915 the Italian Army drafted Padre Pio. But over the next few years, after repeatedly sending him home for poor health and then calling him back into service, the Army gave up: on March 16, 1918, Pio received an honorable discharge. After a few days visiting his family in Pietrelcina, Pio reunited with the Capuchins at San Giovanni Rotondo's Our Lady of Grace Capuchin Friary, which he had first visited in 1916.

The town of San Giovanni Rotondo lies in the "spur" of boot-shaped Italy, in a chain of mountains near the Adriatic Sea. Like Pietrelcina during Pio's childhood, San Giovanni was a small, poor town when Padre Pio first arrived there. Most of its inhabitants were forced to settle for any type of work they could get, most often physical labor that entailed sacrifice and hardship. Few in the town could read, write, or afford "luxuries" like new clothing. The road to the Capuchin friary, according to one of Pio's biographers, was "an impractical, narrow cattle track . . . full of stones and potholes. During the winter it was covered with mud and puddles of water, and in the summer it was infested with serpents and vipers."[3]

The Stigmata

Eight years before receiving the visible, bleeding wounds of Christ in 1918, Pio received a "temporary" stigmata. The unusual red marks, which appeared on his hands and side while he was in Pietrelcina recovering from a long illness, did not bleed. Nevertheless, they caused him constant, extreme pain. Too embarrassed to show them to anyone, Pio hid the stigmata even from his mother. Finally, on September 7, 1910, after bearing those wounds for perhaps only a few months, he showed the marks to Pietrelcina's priest, Fr. Salvatore Panullo. Fr. Panullo sent him to a physician, who could find no natural cause for Pio's pain.

A few days later, Padre Pio again visited Fr. Panullo and told him that although he wanted to suffer all of the physical pain of the marks in reparation for the sins of humanity, he did not want anyone to see them. He wanted to bear all physical pain in secret and, in doing so, to fulfill the words of St. Paul, "to complete what is lacking in Christ's afflictions for the sake of his body, that is, the church" (Colossians 1:24). During his second visit to Fr. Panullo, Pio asked the priest to pray with him for Jesus to take away the physical signs of the wounds but to leave the intense pain of them. At first, the visible signs of the temporary stigmata disappeared, only to return and then disappear again.

On November 29, 1910, Padre Pio wrote to his superior, Fr. Benedetto Nardella, asking permission to offer himself to Jesus as a "victim" for the salvation of sinners and for the holy souls in purgatory. Pio knew that Jesus would accept his sufferings to help atone for the sins of the living and of those in purgatory. Without a doubt, Pio believed that the Lord wanted him to make this lifelong sacrifice of himself. In his reply to Pio, Fr. Benedetto heartily agreed to his request.

The temporary stigmata may have been a sign that Jesus had indeed accepted Padre Pio's offering of himself as a "victim" for sinners. After Pio's return to San Giovanni, the Lord again seemed to accept him as a "victim" by giving him—in the friary church on September 20, 1918—the permanent, visible, ever-bleeding stigmata on Pio's hands, feet, and side. After Pio received these wounds of Christ, his fame and reputation for holiness spread rapidly over Italy and around the world. The number of pilgrims to San Giovanni swelled, gradually transforming the unknown little village into today's modern bustling town, famous throughout the world. Most in San Giovanni agree that the name and holiness of Padre Pio brought about this remarkable transformation.

His Enemies

In spite of his holiness, spiritual gifts, and unquenchable love for God and neighbor, Pio had enemies. In 1919, a few well-known priests and theologians told the Vatican that Pio was a fraud. Among Pio's enemies, the psychologist and theologian Fr. Agostino Gemelli told Rome that Pio's hysterical mind had caused the stigmata. The archbishop of Manfredonia, Pasquale Gagliardi, swore that Pio had inflicted the stigmata himself and that demons possessed Pio.

Within the same time period, the media printed rumors that Pio's confreres at the San Giovanni Rotondo friary were making money promoting Padre Pio to the faithful who flocked to him for counseling, confession, intercession, and healing. When Pio's enemies, including Gagliardi, recommended that the Vatican prohibit him from continuing his ministries at San Giovanni, Pope Benedict XV would not agree to it. In fact, as long as Benedict lived, he and other top church authorities staunchly supported Pio and protected him from his enemies.

Unfortunately, in January 1922 the pope died from complications due to pneumonia, and the archbishop of Milan, Achille

Ratti, succeeded him as Pope Pius XI. Immediately, Gagliardi visited the new pope and made scathing allegations—proved years later to be lies—about Padre Pio. Among other claims, Gagliardi denounced Pio as possessed by demons. Finally, by the spring of 1922, as a result of Gagliardi's "war" against Pio, Pius XI ordered the Vatican's Holy Office (the title used before Vatican II for the Congregation for the Doctrine of the Faith) to investigate the matter. Relying on doubtful witnesses like Gagliardi, the Holy Office ordered Fr. Giuseppantonio Bussolari, the Capuchin minister general, to transfer Padre Pio to a distant friary (to be chosen by the Capuchins). But when the people of San Giovanni found out about the proposed transfer, they—along with some of the local civic authorities—threatened violence against anyone who might try to take away their beloved priest, and so Fr. Giuseppantonio backed down and did not transfer Pio.

Nevertheless, Padre Pio's enemies continued to bombard church officials with false accusations against him. Finally, in July 1923, Fr. Giuseppantonio decided to transfer Pio. But when one of Pio's local devotees (today known by sources only as "Donato") threatened to murder Padre Pio if he were transferred, church authorities reconsidered and suspended the order.

In April 1931, when news reached San Giovanni that church authorities again were planning to transfer Padre Pio, the citizens of the town protested. Believing that the priest belonged exclusively to them, hundreds of the townspeople rallied around his monastery and created such an uproar that news of their demonstration reached the Vatican. That news was all Gagliardi and a few other church authorities needed to get Rome to take action against the innocent Pio.

On June 11, 1931, the Holy Office sent an order to the San Giovanni monastery that forbade Padre Pio to practice his priestly duties, except for saying daily Mass. Even then, he was only allowed to celebrate Mass privately in the monastery's inner chapel. The news caused Pio tremendous pain, but he submitted to the will of the church, believing that in doing so he was submitting to the will of God. This sacrifice lasted two years, during which Padre Pio continually offered his suffering to God for the sins of the world and for the souls in purgatory.

Until March 1933, Pope Pius XI had based the restrictions of Padre Pio on information provided by Gagliardi and other authorities who were biased against Pio. However, that month, Pope Pius decided to send two of his personally chosen officials to San Giovanni to investigate Pio. On July 14, 1933, after these two officials gave the pope a favorable report concerning the priest, Pope Pius reversed the ban he had placed on Pio.

When the good news reached the San Giovanni friary and the superior told Padre Pio and his fellow friars in the dining hall, tears filled Pio's eyes, and he asked the superior to relay his gratitude to the pope.[4]

Pio's Spirituality

Thousands of people from all over the world sought the fruits of Padre Pio's spiritual life. His faithfulness to prayer and to adoration of Christ in the Eucharist led his superiors at Our Lady of Grace Capuchin Friary to ask Pio for spiritual advice. His emphasis on the Mass and confession led thousands of people to new life in Jesus Christ.

Padre Pio expressed his spirituality by devotion to the Eucharist, to Mary, to the church, and to the pope. He also nurtured a tender devotion to guardian angels, the saints, and the souls in purgatory. Pio frequently meditated before the Blessed Sacrament in the tabernacle. Pio's words hint at the depth of his devotion: "My heart feels drawn by a higher force each morning before I am united with Jesus in the Blessed Sacrament."[5]

The Holy Spirit gave Padre Pio many spiritual gifts, which God used to bring countless souls to Christ. For example, in the confessional, Pio often recited penitents' sins before they confessed them. If someone hid a deadly sin from him, Pio would remind him about it. The penitent would repent, receive forgiveness, and joyfully place himself in God's hands. Pio also prophesied, counseled, healed, and performed miracles. He could bilocate—appear in more than one place at a time—and he had the gift of perfume that emanated from him. "It is a sign that I am close to the soul [who experiences it]," he explained to one of his brothers.[6]

But what most influenced people to turn to God were Pio's inner qualities, not his visibly spectacular gifts. What drew people to the Lord were Pio's uncompromising adherence to his principles; his speaking the truth at all times to all people, even if the truth might not be easy to hear; and his unwavering humility and obedience. When people met Pio, they realized that he was a man of God. This made them want the same holiness and peace he possessed. They saw how Pio trusted God with a childlike faith in spite of his constant physical sufferings, including the pain of his stigmata. Most of all, Pio's visitors sensed his unrelenting and ever-growing love of God and neighbor.

How did Pio's love for God manifest itself? His constant determination to help those suffering—physically, spiritually, and emotionally—demonstrated his love. With only a small, rudimentary hospital serving San Giovanni in 1918, Padre Pio decided to build a large, modern hospital, despite the mercilessly rocky ground that was part of the landscape. Pio's faithful friend and caregiver, Fr. Alessio Parente, knew that the saint's constant suffering helped him to empathize with and love all who suffered. "And this great love of [Padre Pio's]," wrote Fr. Alessio, "has been immortalized in the shape of his hospital."[7]

Pio's spirituality is captured in the fifteen meditations that are included in *Praying with Padre Pio*. Here is a short summary of the themes that will be covered:

1 Holy Gift of Prayer

Padre Pio's spirituality was fostered by continual prayer, including the Mass, the rosary, meditation on Christ's passion, and contemplation. "If you can speak to the Lord," wrote Pio, "do so. . . . If you are unable to speak . . . don't worry. In the ways of the Lord, stop in your room . . . and pay him homage. He will see this and will be pleased with your patience; he will favor your silence."[8]

During the Second World War, in response to a request by Pope Pius XII, Padre Pio urged all his followers (often referred to as his "spiritual children") to form prayer groups to pray for the world. Padre Pio prayer groups now number in the thousands throughout the world.

2 Confession and Forgiveness

Pio's gifts in the confessional reflect the grace of this sacrament available for those who practice it. Penitents who approached Pio in the confessional discovered that he could "simply, clearly, and compassionately tell them how they stood with God. . . . The greatest proof of Pio's effectiveness, not to mention his sanctity, was that through his ministry lives were changed."[9]

3 God's Presence

Pio urged his followers to always acknowledge the presence of God. "Hold resolutely to the comforting thought," said Pio, "that God is with you all the time and will never abandon you."[10]

Emmanuel

4. God Is Love

"The pivot of perfection is love," said Pio. "He who lives in love lives in God because 'God is love' [1 John 4:8]."[11] By heroically sacrificing everything to bring people to salvation, Padre Pio showed them the face of God.

5. Heavenly Obedience

Whether advising a priest, a religious, or a layperson, Padre Pio stressed obedience to one's "superiors." The church and Scripture held top priority in his personal practice of obedience. "Where there is no obedience," said Pio, "there is no virtue."[12]

6. Jesus Suffers with You

Padre Pio urged everyone to accept their daily crosses and thereby obtain blessings through suffering for themselves and for others. "He teaches and repeats that 'the cross,' whatever name it is given and whatever painful form it takes in life, will always . . . be the identity card of souls chosen by the heavenly Father."[13]

7. Jesus in the Eucharist

Pio continually stressed the presence of Jesus in the Eucharist and the strength we can gain by spending time with God before the tabernacle. "We must always have courage. If some spiritual listlessness comes upon us, let us run to the feet of

Jesus in the Blessed Sacrament, place ourselves in the midst of the heavenly perfumes, and we will undoubtedly regain our strength."[14]

The Passion of Jesus, No Greater Love

Pio's spirituality focused primarily on the passion of Christ. Pio encouraged all to embrace their sufferings, offering them to God for the salvation of souls, including their own. He wanted us to follow Paul's example: "I am now rejoicing in my sufferings for your sake, and in my flesh I am completing what is lacking in Christ's afflictions for the sake of his body, that is, the church" (Colossians 1:24).

True Holiness

Believing that true holiness was nurtured in a soul by the action of the Holy Spirit, Padre Pio encouraged his followers to remain open and humble, allowing God to work in their souls.

Holy Angels Smile at Us

Throughout his life, Padre Pio had visions of and conversations with his guardian angel. Pio said his guardian angel helped him to love and obey God, and he urged everyone to develop a relationship with their own holy angel.

11

Humility and Simplicity

Pio's spirituality stressed the need for humility and simplicity. "Be humble with others, since 'God opposes the proud and gives grace to the humble' (James 4:6). The more that graces and favors grow in your soul, the more you should humble yourself and always maintain the humility of our heavenly mother who, the very instant she became the mother of God, declared herself to be the servant and handmaid of the same God."[15] Pio encouraged all to practice simplicity by becoming "like little children" (Matthew 18:3). He wanted all to follow Christ's example, who counted as nothing the riches, esteem, and values of this world.

12

Trusting Only in Jesus

Enduring almost-constant physical, emotional, and spiritual pain, Pio still placed all his trust and hope in Christ. "I do not know what will happen to me," said Pio. "I only know one thing for certain; the Lord will never fall short of his promises."[16]

13

Mary

Knowing from personal experience how Mary's heart ached for all of God's children still struggling against sin and evil, Pio said, "May this most dear mother unite us so closely with Jesus that we may never allow ourselves to be enraptured or lured away."[17]

(14)

Fear Not, Worry Not

Echoing Christ's own words not to be fearful or to worry (Luke 12:17, 22), Pio said, "Do not anticipate the problems of this life with apprehension, but rather with a perfect hope that God, to whom you belong, will free you from them accordingly. . . . He will help you in all events . . . so don't worry."[18]

(15)

Joy in the Lord

Knowing that believers could find joy in the love of God, Pio said, "Love has as its close relatives joy and peace. Joy is born of happiness at possessing what we love."[19]

PIO FOR TODAY

"Prayer," said Pio, "is the best weapon we have. It is a key that opens God's heart."[20] Using the meditations in this book, we can confidently embrace Pio as our spiritual mentor and as our guide in prayer.

On August 20, 2005, during World Youth Day, Pope Benedict XVI invited all youth to get to know Padre Pio so they could learn "what it is to adore and what it means to live according to the teaching of . . . Jesus Christ."[21] As you pray through the meditations in this book, may you come to a greater understanding of Jesus and his teachings, and may that lead you to greater adoration of him each day.

HIGHLIGHTS OF PADRE PIO'S LIFE

1887: Born Francesco Forgione in Pietrelcina, Italy.

1903: Begins novitiate at Capuchin Friary, Morcone, as Fra (Brother) Pio.

1909: Ordained deacon in friary chapel at Morcone.

1910: Ordained priest at Cathedral of Benevento.

1910–1915: Receives temporary invisible stigmata.

1915: Drafted into Italian Army. Granted one year's leave for poor health.

1916: Returns to Army, but soon receives six-month leave for poor health.

1918: Honorably discharged from Army because of poor health. Returns to San Giovanni Rotondo friary where he receives the visible stigmata.

1931: Vatican prohibits Padre Pio from saying Mass in public and from having any contact whatsoever with the public.

1933: Pope Pius XI reverses the ban.

1940: Padre Pio forms the first of his hundreds of worldwide prayer groups.

1947: Construction begins on his hospital, Home for the Relief of Suffering.

1956: Inauguration of Padre Pio's Home for the Relief of Suffering.

1960: Fiftieth anniversary of Padre Pio's priesthood.

1968: Fiftieth anniversary of Padre Pio's visible stigmata. Dies on September 23.

1997: Proclaimed Venerable by Pope John Paul II.

1999: Beatified by Pope John Paul II.

2002: Canonized by Pope John Paul II as Saint Pio of Pietrelcina.

1. Gerardo Di Flumeri, *The Mystery of the Cross in Padre Pio of Pietrelcina*, (San Giovanni Rotondo, Italy: Our Lady of Grace Capuchin Friary, 1977), p. 9.

2. Dorothy M. Gaudiose, *Padre Pio* (New Jersey: Westwood Printing, n.d.), p. 5.

3. Alberto D'Apolito, *Padre Pio of Pietrelcina* (San Giovanni Rotondo, Italy: Our Lady of Grace Capuchin Friary, 1986), p. 56.

4. C. Bernard Ruffin, *Padre Pio: The True Story, Revised and Expanded* (Huntington, IN: Our Sunday Visitor Publishing Division, Our Sunday Visitor, Inc., 1991), pp. 181–236.

5. Padre Pio, *Letters*, vol. 1, 2nd ed., ed. Gerardo Di Flumeri (San Giovanni Rotondo, Italy: Our Lady of Grace Capuchin Friary, 2001), p. 246.

6. Capuchin Friars Minor, *The Charisms of Padre Pio: Calendar 2006* (San Giovanni Rotondo, Italy: Our Lady of Grace Capuchin Friary, 2005), inside front cover.

7. Alessio Parente, *Padre Pio: Our Good Samaritan* (San Giovanni Rotondo, Italy: Our Lady of Grace Capuchin Friary, 1990), pp. 57–58.

8. Padre Pio, *Letters*, vol. 3, 2nd ed., ed. Gerardo Di Flumeri (San Giovanni Rotondo, Italy: Our Lady of Grace Capuchin Friary, 2001), p. 991.

9. Gaudiose, *Padre Pio*, p. 1.

10. Padre Pio, *Letters*, vol. 2, 3rd ed., ed. Gerardo Di Flumeri (San Giovanni Rotondo, Italy: Our Lady of Grace Capuchin Friary, 2002), p. 76.

11. Frederico Abresch, *The Voice of Padre Pio* (San Giovanni Rotondo, Italy: Rewarded Printing Shop, 1954), p. 5.

12. Abresch, *The Voice of Padre Pio*, p. 13.

13. Pio, *Letters,* vol. 3, p. lxvi.

14. Pio, *Letters,* vol. 3, p. 507.

15. Pio, *Letters,* vol. 3, pp. 51–52.

16. Pio, *Letters,* vol. 1, p. 382.

17. Pio, *Letters,* vol. 1, p. 677.

18. Pio, *Letters,* vol. 3, p. 730.

19. Pio, *Letters,* vol. 2, p. 214.

20. Alessio Parente, *Our Lady of Grace Prayer Book* (San Giovanni Rotondo, Italy: Our Lady of Grace Capuchin Friary, 1988), p. 7.

21. Francesco Colacelli, "An Affinity That Continues," in *The Voice of Padre Pio*, vol. 35, ed. Capuchin Friars (San Giovanni Rotondo, Italy: Capuchin Friars, Nov.–Dec., 2005), p. 3.

Holy Gift of Prayer

Theme: "The holy gift of prayer is placed in the right hand of the Savior," said Padre Pio. "And in the measure in which you will be empty of yourself . . . and will keep rooting yourself in holy humility, the Lord will continue to communicate himself to your heart."[1]

 Opening Prayer: Lord, keep my heart and soul always communicating with you, even when my mind and body must focus on my duties. Amen.

ABOUT PIO

Padre Pio continually communicated with God. His prayer included daily Mass, the rosary, meditation on the passion of Christ, and contemplation, during which he silently adored God. "[Prayer is the] true ladder which unites the earth to the heavens," said Pio. "We will discover that humility, contrition, and prayer make the distance between mankind and God disappear and act in such a way that God descends to mankind and mankind ascends to God, so that they end up understanding, loving, and possessing one another."[2]

Padre Pio's life of prayer began in early childhood. As a child, he prayed whenever he could, whether kneeling at home on the stone floor, at church before the tabernacle, or with his family during their daily rosary. As Pio grew closer to God, he looked for opportunities to pray more and more. In the middle of trials and suffering of any kind, Pio found his comfort in prayer.

A close friend of Padre Pio's, Fr. Agostino Daniele of San Marco in Lamis, wrote in his diary in February 1944, twenty-four years before Pio's death, "The thought of God is habitual in him. He lives his interior life like the saints did. Even when he talks with [us], we are aware of the fact that his spirit is lifted towards God."[3]

In 1999, after beatifying Padre Pio, Pope John Paul II said about him,

> He longed for many souls to join him in prayer. "Pray," he used to say. "Pray to the Lord with me because the whole world needs prayers. And every day, when your heart especially feels the loneliness of life, pray; pray to the Lord together."[4]

Because he suffered physically, emotionally, and spiritually every day, Padre Pio cared deeply about all who suffered. He helped them understand the value of their suffering and crosses. In his encounters with penitents and those who sought his intercession for healing, Pio emphasized the value in offering suffering to Jesus as "prayer" for the salvation of souls. He believed that the best form of charity was prayer, and stressed that the most effective way to help the sick was to pray for them.

Through Padre Pio's prayers, healings also occurred. One well-documented healing concerned a young girl, Gemma di Giordi. She was born blind and without pupils. When her grandmother heard about the power of Pio's prayers, she took Gemma to San Giovanni Rotondo, where they attended a Mass said by Padre Pio. After the Mass, Pio put his hand on Gemma and asked Christ's mother to intercede for the girl. Only minutes later a startled Gemma said she could now see. Months later, a well-known eye specialist declared that Gemma could indeed see, even though she *still* had no pupils.[5]

Padre Pio's prayer life embraced fervent devotion to Mary, the mother of God. Day and night, Pio recited the rosary, concentrating on the gospel scenes of each mystery. He wanted everyone to say the rosary at least once a day, meditating on the humility, power, love, and salvation that Christ, through Mary, brings to each person who prays. Biographer Francesco Napolitano noted,

Padre Pio's love became an endless . . . prayer. He always carried [the rosary] in his hand or on his arm. . . . He had other rosaries under the pillow of his bed and on the bureau in his cell. He called the rosary his "weapon." One night when he was sick in bed, he was unable to find his rosary. He called Father Onorato and said, "Young man, get me my weapon."[6]

Padre Pio practiced a special devotion to each of the three divine Persons of the Trinity. He particularly welcomed God the Father into the center of his heart and allowed him to do as he pleased in his soul. In a letter to one of his "spiritual children," those people who considered themselves disciples of Pio, he said, "Continue to serve the infinite goodness of this heavenly Father with ever-increasing sincerity and sweetness of spirit because with much love and sweetness he has invited and called you to himself."[7]

Since he desired, in all things, to please his heavenly Father, Pio enjoyed praying the prayer taught to us by Jesus, the Our Father. At his last Mass, on September 22, 1968, he sang the Our Father. Later that day in his small cell, he recited the same prayer as he waited for the Lord to take him "home." Throughout his life, Pio sought to love and worship the Father according to these words of Jesus: "True worshipers will worship the Father in spirit and truth, for the Father seeks such as these to worship him" (John 4:23).

A master of prayer, Pio died just as he had lived, with the names of Jesus and Mary on his lips.

Pause: How does Padre Pio's intense life of prayer inspire you to pray?

PIO'S WORDS

Never fear the snares of evil, because even though they may be harsh, they will never succeed in displacing a soul who keeps attached to the cross. Be vigilant and fortify yourself more and more with prayer and with the beautiful virtue of humility.[8]

Rise above yourself with spontaneous short prayers and aspirations of the heart, which are true, continual prayers.[9]

Blessed be the Lord for his great goodness. Blessed be his great mercy. Eternal praise be to such tender and loving compassion.[10]

I exhort you to approach God with filial trust. . . . He loves you and you return his love as best you can. . . . You must confide in him.[11]

Pray, hope, and don't worry.[12]

REFLECTION

When we study Pio's life, we discover when, how, and why we should pray. As to *when* to pray, Pio wants us to follow Paul's advice: "Pray without ceasing" (1 Thessalonians 5:17). *How* should we pray? Pio recommended private prayer (see Matthew 6:6) as well as family and community prayer (see 18:20). *Why should we pray?* Padre Pio believed that prayer is our best weapon against evil and that it can actually open God's heart to us.

We do not always need to say formal prayers to God. Padre Pio said that simply lifting up our hearts to him in short, spontaneous prayer can please God just as much as long, formal prayers. When we have no words at all to say to the Lord, when we are so burdened by work, worries, and suffering that we *cannot* pray, simply placing ourselves humbly and silently in God's presence will please the Lord.

Do you think that our omnipotent Creator could not possibly want to listen to "insignificant" you? Pio believed that not only does God want to listen to you, God *longs* for you to come to him in prayer. "Let me see your face, let me hear your voice," God says to you in Solomon 2:14. And Jesus implores you, "Come to me" (Matthew 11:28).

❧ Padre Pio often told those who sought his encouragement and prayers, "Pray, hope, and don't worry." Find a quiet spot in which to sit. If you cannot find one, retreat to that quiet space within yourself where God resides. Breathe deeply and close your eyes. As you slowly inhale, silently say, "Pray, hope, and don't worry." As you slowly exhale, silently repeat, "Pray, hope, and don't worry." Repeat this exercise for several minutes. As you do, visualize yourself completely supported by God's gentle, loving arms. Practice this exercise each day and especially during times of stress and suffering.

❦ Read Mark 11:24: "So I tell you, whatever you ask for in prayer, believe that you have received it, and it will be yours." Consider how you usually pray. Do you pray with hesitation or confidence? Do you pray believing that God really *can* meet your needs? God never fails to answer our prayers; he just doesn't always answer them in the manner in which we would prefer. Are you ready to accept whatever answer God gives you? Resolve to pray today with confidence and humility, knowing that God alone knows what is best for you and for all those for whom you pray. *"God our Father knows best!"*

❦ If possible, go for a ten-minute walk or lie on a soft carpet or grassy spot. Breathe deeply and look up and smile as if you were smiling at God. But rather than petitioning the Lord, spend this time thanking him for everything and everyone in your life, and even for those elements of your life—including people—that do not please you. If possible, repeat this exercise once a day.

GOD'S WORD

[Jesus said,] "So I say to you, Ask, and it will be given you; search, and you will find; knock, and the door will be opened for you. For everyone who asks receives, and everyone who searches finds, and for everyone who knocks, the door will be opened." (Luke 11:9-10)

Closing Prayer: Dear Lord, I often neglect prayer, claiming that I am too busy. By the power and love of your Holy Spirit, keep me praying always and thanking you in all things, even for my trials. "Rejoice always, pray without ceasing, give thanks in all circumstances; for this is the will of God in Christ Jesus for you" (1 Thessalonians 5:16-18).

1. Frederico Abresch, *The Voice of Padre Pio* (San Giovanni Rotondo, Italy: Rewarded Printing Shop, 1954), p. 17.

2. Padre Pio, *Letters*, vol. 3, 2nd ed., ed. Gerardo Di Flumeri (San Giovanni Rotondo, Italy: Our Lady of Grace Capuchin Friary, 2001), p. 98.

3. Alessio Parente, *Padre Pio: Our Good Samaritan* (San Giovanni Rotondo, Italy: Our Lady of Grace Capuchin Friary, 1990), p. 154.

4. Gennaro Preziuso, *The Life of Padre Pio: Between the Altar and the Confessional* (New York: Alba House, 2000), p. 235.

5. Clarice Bruno, "The Blind See," in *Padre Pio the Wonder Worker*

(New Bedford, MA: Franciscan Friars of the Immaculate, n.d.), pp. 113–14.

6. Francesco Napolitano, *Padre Pio of Pietrelcina* (San Giovanni Rotondo, Italy: Edizioni "Voce di Padre Pio," 1979), p. 217.

7. Pio, *Letters,* vol. 3, p. 313.

8. Pio, *Letters,* vol. 3, p. 97.

9. Pio, *Letters,* vol. 3, p. 270.

10. Padre Pio, *Letters,* vol. 1, 2nd ed., ed. Gerardo Di Flumeri (San Giovanni Rotondo, Italy: Our Lady of Grace Capuchin Friary, 1984), p. 730.

11. Pio, *Letters,* vol. 3, p. 81.

12. Stella Maris Lilley, *On the Road with Padre Pio* (San Giovanni Rotondo, Italy: Edizioni Padre Pio da Pietrelcina, n.d.), p. 45.

MEDITATION TWO
Confession and forgiveness

Theme: "The gates of heaven are open for all creatures," said Pio. "Remember Mary Magdalene. The mercy of God is infinitely greater than your malice."[1]

Opening Prayer: Merciful Lord, when I sin, and when shame threatens to keep me from asking for your forgiveness, remind me of how you forgave Mary Magdalene. Then I will gladly confess and ask forgiveness, and you will heal my soul, and like Mary Magdalene, I will love you more than ever before (see Luke 7:47-48).

Lk 8:1-3 "Accompanying him were the Twelve and some women who had been cured of evil spirits and infirmities; mary, called Magdalene, from whom seven demons had gone out, Joanna

ABOUT PIO

As did Christ, Padre Pio wanted to reach out to sinners, not just to those who were already leading holy lives. "For I have come to call not the righteous but sinners" (Matthew 9:13). When one of his followers complained about her weaknesses, fearing that they might cause her to sin, Pio assured her that the Lord wanted to dwell in her, weaknesses and all:

Jesus is on your breast; he is within your heart. Isn't this enough to make you fight valiantly [the spiritual war]?

41

my prayer has long been, "Lord, keep me close to You no matter what happens and no matter what doesn't happen,"

Isn't Jesus the beginning and the end of all we could desire? One thing alone is necessary: to be close to him, and you are! How happy you must be to be close to Jesus and to be held so tightly to him. You need do no more than what you are already doing; love this divine goodness and abandon yourself to his arms and heart.[2]

Fr. John Schug, OFM Cap, Pio's biographer and fellow Capuchin priest, said that in the confessional, Padre Pio was a "surgeon of the soul." The confessional, according to Schug, was where Pio did his "real work." When perplexed about how to touch and penetrate the hearts and souls of the people who came to him, Schug said that Pio would, in effect, ask Jesus, "How can I reach these souls? How can I really get to them, to crack through that exterior, that façade which they have built up through their egotism?"[3]

God answered Padre Pio's prayer by giving him the gift of reading souls. Often, when his penitents stepped into his confessional, knelt down, made the Sign of the Cross, and said, "Bless me, Father, for I have sinned," he would recite their sins to them as if he had read their consciences—even before they said a word. In 1958, ten years before Padre Pio's death, biographer Nesta de Robeck shared his experiences of what it was like in Our Lady of Grace church when Padre Pio heard confessions: "Something unspecified makes people want to go to confession [to Pio], and they may then have to listen to Pio's exact recitation of their most intimate sins and affairs; this has happened—and happens—to many."[4]

John McCaffery, another biographer and friend who knew him well, said this about Pio's role as confessor:

Padre Pio's day revolved chiefly around his confessional. And it is, I believe, as a confessor more than for anything else that he would wish to be remembered. Hour after hour, day after day, week after week, he sat there, for fifty long years.

He had his Rule to follow; he was Spiritual Director of the Community; he had his helpers to listen to and advise on the Hospital [which he built in San Giovanni]; he daily received a massive amount of correspondence. . . . On top of that, he bore . . . the wounds and sufferings of Christ.

Even without the long fatiguing hours of concentration in the confessional . [Pio's] was an existence that the greatest human strength could not have stood up to for long. It was a life which, without his complete immersion in God, would have been absolutely impossible to bear. But for fifty years, he bore it all in the intense heat and bitter cold of [San Giovanni].

How was he as a confessor? All things to all people. . . . All sincere men and women were at once enveloped in the mantle of his sanctity. They came away not only cleansed, but . . . more keenly aware of what sin really meant.[5]

Padre Pio urged penitents not to give up when they sinned. They should not waste time chastising themselves, but rather tell the Lord that they are sorry for their sins and then pick themselves up and continue in holiness. He did not want his penitents to remain mired in guilt after confessing their sins, but instead to follow Peter's example. After Peter denied the Lord, he wept in repentance, and after Christ's resurrection, Peter declared his love for Jesus (see Mark 14:72 and John 21:15-17). Pio advised his penitents not to despair over their sins like Judas who, after betraying Jesus, went out and hanged himself (see Matthew 27:5).

After a penitent had asked God's forgiveness and resolved to sin no more, Padre Pio would tell them: "Fortify yourself with prayer, humility, and unlimited trust in divine help. Abandon yourself as a beloved child of the heavenly Father, in his most loving arms, and do not fear the war waged against you by the evil one."[6]

Many people in Pio's time, like today, refused to believe in hell. Once when a wealthy, lavishly dressed woman told Pio that she did not believe in hell, he said, "You will believe it when you get there."[7]

A woman once confided to Padre Pio that fear overtook her whenever she thought about her sinful nature and her weaknesses. He told her not to fear, adding, "Let us humble ourselves deeply and confess that if God were not our breastplate and shield, we should at once be pierced by every kind of sin. This is why we must invariably keep ourselves in God by persevering in our spiritual exercises and learning to serve God at our own expense."[8] Pio found confession essential for himself, too. Knowing his own need to be forgiven and to continually reconcile with God and with those around him, Padre Pio urged people to confess their sins on a regular basis. To those who thought God could not possibly forgive them their most grievous sins, he always said, "The mercy of God is infinitely greater than your malice."

Pause: Have you committed any sins that you do not believe God will forgive?

PIO'S WORDS

"Once, in a group of women who were waiting for Padre Pio to pass, there happened to be one of [loose] morals. Padre Pio, with his supernatural intuition, spoke gently, 'Will the one among you who has had the courage to follow Mary Magdalene in sin, please have the strength to follow her in penance? Anyone who has fallen in mud can still be saved if he has the will.' Upon hearing these words, one of the group fell to her knees, asking forgiveness and promising to start a new life. . . . 'Be calm, my dear,' said Padre Pio. 'God's compassion is unlimited, and the blood of Jesus Christ washes away all the sins of the world.'"[9]

> *When someone asked Pio if God loves the repentant sinner as much as the innocent soul, Padre Pio said yes and encouraged penitents to get to know intimately "this Lover. He is the One who is never angry with those who offend him."* [10]

REFLECTION

We all want to lead a holy life, but temptations threaten to defeat us. Why does God permit those temptations in our lives, even after we have confessed and promised to sin no more? Padre Pio said, "No chosen soul is free from temptations. . . . Therefore, take heart. . . . In times of great struggle and extreme weakness, turn to prayer, trust in God, and you will never be overcome by temptation."[11]

Pio's use of the word "chosen" might puzzle us. If God has *chosen* us to forever love and serve him, how can temptations help us to do that? Pio always explained that *because* we are chosen, God wants us to follow Christ's example. God wants us to accept our spiritual as well as physical trials and to allow them to help us grow in holiness, humility, and love, in imitation of our Lord.

But what should we do if we succumb to temptation and sin? No matter what sins we have committed, no matter how many times we have committed them, if we turn to Jesus and confess our sins, he will forgive us and "cleanse us from all unrighteousness" (1 John 1:9). Not only can we—at any time and any place—ask Christ for his forgiveness in our informal confessions, he will forgive and heal us in a particularly powerful way when we turn to him for forgiveness in the Sacrament of Reconciliation.

From Padre Pio's life, we see that he welcomed *every* repentant sinner and encouraged that sinner to lead a holy life. Like our good shepherd, Jesus, Pio longed for even the "black sheep" to turn to God, repent, and forever follow Christ. Pio assured everyone that up until the moment we have breathed our last breath, if we turn to God and ask his forgiveness, our merciful Lord will forgive us and welcome us into his heavenly kingdom.

꧁ Whenever you fear that God will not forgive you, meditate on *why* Christ suffered and sacrificed his life for you. Let Jesus' sacrifice convince you of his love and mercy, of his longing to forgive you.

In hundreds of letters to superiors and spiritual children, Padre Pio declared that Christ would never allow temptation to defeat them if they trusted in him. As St. Paul wrote, "No testing has overtaken you that is not common to everyone. God is faithful, and he will not let you be tested beyond your strength, but with the testing he will also provide the way out so that you may be able to endure it" (1 Corinthians 10:13).

When temptation comes your way, do you trust Christ to protect you? To prepare and fortify yourself for the inevitable temp-

"Regret, guilt & shame are obstacles in our relationship with God."

tations that will threaten you throughout your life, memorize 1 Corinthians 10:13. Let the words saturate your mind, heart, and soul. Call the verse to mind whenever you feel threatened.

Like God, Pio does not want you to remain mired in guilt and shame once you have confessed your sins. Pio said, "Hasten confidently to the tribunal [of mercy], where [God] is constantly waiting for us. Although we are aware of our inability to repay him, let us not doubt that he has solemnly pardoned our errors. Let us place a tombstone on them just as the Lord did."[12] Consider carefully for a few moments what Pio meant by "place a tombstone on them." If you cling to your guilt and shame, would this insult or sadden God? Spend some time reflecting on how your refusal to accept Christ's joyful forgiveness and cleansing of your heart and soul might cause you spiritual harm.

Do you need to let go of any hard feelings you harbor toward someone? Who do you need to forgive? Recall the prayer Jesus taught us, the Our Father, which says that we must forgive as the Father forgives us. Write a list of the people you need to forgive. Create a litany by writing something like the following for each name: "I forgive William for the rude remarks he made to me. Thank you, merciful God." "I forgive Nancy for bragging about her accomplishments. Thank you, merciful God." When you finish writing your litany, read it aloud to God, asking the Holy Spirit to help you truly forgive each person on your list.

Then shred, cut up, or burn the list as a symbolic gesture that you have forgiven all those on your list.

GOD'S WORD

The next day [John the Baptist] saw Jesus coming toward him and declared, "Here is the Lamb of God who takes away the sin of the world!" (John 1:29)

Closing Prayer: Lord, I am sorry for all my sins. Please forgive me and help me to sin no more. Lamb of God, you take away the sins of the world; have mercy on us. Lamb of God, you take away the sins of the world; have mercy on us. Lamb of God, you take away the sins of the world; grant us peace. Amen.

1. Frederico Abresch, *The Voice of Padre Pio* (San Giovanni Rotondo, Italy: Rewarded Printing Shop, 1954), pp. 35–36.

2. Padre Pio, *Letters*, vol. 3, 2nd ed., ed. Gerardo Di Flumeri (San Giovanni Rotondo, Italy: Our Lady of Grace Capuchin Friary, 2001), p. 180.

3. John A. Schug, *A Padre Pio Profile* (Petersham, MA: St. Bede's Publications, 1987), p. 67.

4. Nesta De Robeck, *Padre Pio* (Milwaukee: The Bruce Publishing Company, 1958), p. 61.

5. John McCaffery, *The Friar of San Giovanni: Tales of Padre Pio*

(London: Darton, Longman & Todd Ltd, 1983), pp. 56–57.

6. Pio, *Letters,* vol. 3, p. 72.

7. Stella Maris Lilley, *On the Road with Padre Pio* (San Giovanni Rotondo, Italy: Edizioni Padre Pio da Pietrelcina, n.d.), p. 217.

8. Padre Pio, *Letters,* vol. 1, 2nd ed., ed. Gerardo Di Flumeri (San Giovanni Rotondo, Italy: Our Lady of Grace Capuchin Friary, 1984), p. 1020.

9. Francesco Napolitano, *Padre Pio of Pietrelcina* (San Giovanni Rotondo, Italy: Edizioni "Voce di Padre Pio," 1979), pp. 124–25.

10. Pio, *Letters,* vol. 1, p. 357.

11. Pio, *Letters,* vol. 3, pp. 249–50.

12. Alessio Parente, ed., *Have a Good Day* (San Giovanni Rotondo, Italy: Our Lady of Grace Capuchin Friary, 1990), p. 44.

God's Presence

Theme: Pio said, "We are always in the presence of the majesty of God. . . . <u>One thing is necessary, to be near Jesus</u>. . . . Continually live under the eyes of the Good Shepherd and you will walk unharmed through poisoned pastures."[1]

Opening Prayer: "In your presence there is fullness of joy" (Psalm 16:11). Help me, Lord of joy, to always and everywhere practice your presence. Even when I am having difficulty perceiving your presence, help me to frequently lift up a word or phrase that expresses my love and longing for you. Help me to smile at you and acknowledge you at all times.

ABOUT PIO

Padre Pio had an abiding awareness of God's presence in each and every moment of the day, as evidenced by his life of prayer. However, sooner or later, anyone seeking to live in constant awareness of God's presence may experience what Pio and other mystics have called "the dark night of the soul." Those who are in this dark time may feel as if God has abandoned them. Padre Pio knew the desolation of Jesus on the cross: "My God, my God, why have you forsaken me?" (Mark 15:34). On September

4, 1915, Pio wrote about his own dark night of the soul to his superior, Fr. Agostino Daniele:

> My soul and body are pressed down by an enormous weight. . . . The thought of God is what still sustains my soul. The idea that he is everywhere present affords scant consolation to my soul which no longer enjoys the presence of the Beloved and feels the harshness and burden of its own solitude. . . .
>
> All my thoughts tell me that I am far from God and that no healing balm is capable of soothing this cruel wound. No medicine is of any use, nor is there any consolation.[2]

After his dark night finally ended, Padre Pio advised others experiencing the same spiritual darkness to—surprisingly enough—express gratitude to God for allowing them to suffer in this way. For example, when his superior, Fr. Agostino, asked for Pio's advice on how to encourage and console two penitents who were experiencing this dark night of the soul, Pio replied,

> God has plunged their intellect into darkness; their will is set in aridity, their memory in a void, their heart in sorrow and depression, in extreme desolation. All this is very much to be envied, for it all combines to dispose and prepare their hearts to receive the true imprint of the Spirit, which is none other than loving union.

God is with them, and to convince them of this it ought to be sufficient for them to observe that they have the will at all times to devote themselves entirely to God and to perform works in his service and for his honor and glory.[3]

If we find ourselves enveloped by the dark night of the soul, we can do as Padre Pio suggested: "Rejoice in the Lord at the high dignity to which he is raising [you], and have complete trust in the same Lord, like holy Job when God placed him in this state and Job hoped to see light after the darkness" (Job 17:12).[4]

Pause: Reflect on a recent time when you felt surrounded by darkness, far from God's presence. Through what means did God restore you to his divine light?

PIO'S WORDS

When one of his spiritual children feared that God had abandoned her in the middle of her trials, Padre Pio advised,

Courage, I beg you. Pay no attention to the path of trial, but keep your eyes constantly fixed on God who guides you to the heavenly homeland. Why should the soul be despondent? . . . Believe me, Jesus is with you, so what do you fear? Take heart and fear nothing. After you have beseeched the good God to console you, if he is not pleased to do so, think of it no more. Take courage and take on the work of your sanctification on the cross, as if you were never to descend from it, and as if you were never to see the heavens serene again. What do you expect? We must see and speak to God amidst the thunder and the hurricanes. . . .

May Jesus always be with you, and may he continue to sustain you in the extremely harsh and painful trial through which you are passing.[5]

Padre Pio said to someone who kept searching for God but could not seem to find him,

I beg you once again not to worry about this because Jesus is with you, and where he is the Kingdom of God can be found. Your continual aspiring to him should convince you of this. Can Jesus possibly be far from you when you call him, pray to him, seek him, and possess him? How is it possible for divine love to be lacking in you when you, like a deer parched with thirst, hasten to that eternal source of living water? (see Psalm 42:1).[6]

REFLECTION

Sometimes when we seek God, he seems to hide from us. During his own dark night of the soul, Pio felt as if God were pushing him away. Though Pio desired only God, he felt as if God were tormenting him. On February 27, 1916, Pio wrote to his spiritual director, Fr. Agostino, "At certain moments it seems to me that my soul is at the point of grasping God, the object of its desire. . . . The object of my torment suddenly hides from me and, with a hand that I call cruel, pushes me far away from him."[7]

Perhaps you have had a similar experience, when in the total darkness caused by your suffering and trials, you felt as Padre Pio did, that God had pushed you out of his presence and left you to wallow alone in your misery. The next time your troubles, suffering, or pain tempt you to believe that God has deserted you, simply trust along with the psalmist: "Even though I walk through the darkest valley, I fear no evil; for you are with me" (Psalm 23:4). Whatever our feelings, God never leaves us.

🕯 How does God speak to you in your physical, emotional, and spiritual suffering? Does he ask you to accept your sufferings and to offer them up to him for the salvation of souls, perhaps the souls of your family? In your journal or on a blank sheet of paper, write a letter to God about your trials and ask him to help you embrace them and to offer them up.

🕯 Light a candle and meditate on these words of Pio: "Live tranquilly and don't be bewildered in the dark night through which your spirit is passing. Be patient and resigned while awaiting the return of your divine Sun who will soon come to brighten the forest of your spirit."[8] In the recent past, how did your "divine Sun"—Jesus—dispel your inner darkness with his light?

Do you have a favorite place where you like to walk or sit, where you can meditate on God's presence? Go to that place, if you can, or visit it in your imagination—or gaze at a photo of a tranquil place in nature—and meditate on God's presence. Inhale deeply, while you silently and slowly repeat Jesus' promise to you, "I am with you always . . ." (Matthew 28:20). As you slowly exhale, use your imagination to visualize Jesus standing before you, smiling and inviting you to rest in his presence. Repeat this exercise until you feel at peace and relaxed in God's loving presence.

GOD'S WORD

He has said, "I will never leave you or forsake you." So we can say with confidence, "The Lord is my helper; I will not be afraid. What can anyone do to me?" Remember . . . Jesus Christ is the same yesterday and today and forever. (Hebrews 13:5-6, 8)

[Jesus said,] "The kingdom of God is not coming with things that can be observed; nor will they say, 'Look, here it is!' or 'There it is!' For, in fact, the kingdom of God is [within] you." (Luke 17:20-21)

Closing Prayer: Conclude your meditation with the following prayer of Padre Pio. As you pray with Pio, express your need for God's assurance of his presence in the midst of your spiritual darkness:

Lord, for pity's sake, do not permit my poor soul to go astray; never allow my hope to be deluded. Never let me be separated from you, and if I am, at this moment, unknowingly separated from you, then rescue me. Enlighten my mind, O my God, so that I may know myself fully and recognize the great love you have shown me. Allow me to enjoy for all eternity the supreme beauty of your divine countenance. . . . Lord, do not take pleasure in hiding yourself; you know what confusion and tumult this causes in my soul and in my feelings. . . . [Let me know you have not deserted me], Lord, and I will bless the abundance of your mercy.[9]

1. Frederico Abresch, *The Voice of Padre Pio* (San Giovanni Rotondo, Italy: Rewarded Printing Shop, 1954), pp. 43, 48, 52.

2. Padre Pio, *Letters*, vol. 1, 2nd ed., ed. Gerardo Di Flumeri (San Giovanni Rotondo, Italy: Our Lady of Grace Capuchin Friary, 1984), p. 715.

3. Pio, *Letters*, vol. 1, pp. 493–94.

4. Pio, *Letters*, vol. 1, p. 495.

5. Padre Pio, *Letters,* vol. 3, 2nd ed., ed. Gerardo Di Flumeri (San Giovanni Rotondo, Italy: Our Lady of Grace Capuchin Friary, 2001), pp. 263, 629.

6. Pio, *Letters,* vol. 3, p. 107.

7. Pio, *Letters,* vol. 1, p. 835.

8. Pio, *Letters,* vol. 3, p. 492.

9. Pio, *Letters,* vol. 1, pp. 752, 753, 755.

God Is Love

Theme: "The pivot of perfection is love," said Pio. "He who lives in love lives in God, because 'God is love'" (1 John 4:8).[1]

Opening Prayer: Dear Lord, I sometimes wonder how you can possibly love me with all my weaknesses and failings. Grant me the faith to believe in your love for me, and help me to love you with all my being. Inspire me to demonstrate my love for you by loving and caring for all the people you put into my life each day.

ABOUT PIO

Sometimes we think of God as a stern taskmaster, waiting to punish us for any sins we might commit. Or perhaps we are tempted to think that God's only intention is to control us. But Scripture says that God is love (see 1 John 4:8). Love is not controlling, and it is not vengeful. Although we sometimes find it difficult to believe, God loves us despite our weaknesses, sins, and failings.

When we realize the immensity of God's unconditional love, we can only respond with love and gratitude. Padre Pio recognized and experienced the overwhelming love of God, and gratitude flowed from his heart to Jesus for his saving work on the cross. Pio demonstrated his love and gratitude by allowing God to use him to reach out to humanity in love and to work for the salvation of all. The priest did not merely talk and write about love; he showed his love through good works.

Today in San Giovanni Rotondo stands one of Padre Pio's tangible works of love: the huge, modern hospital, Home for the Relief of Suffering, which he envisioned and then supervised to completion. But how could a priest who owned nothing and lived in a monastery in a barren region of impoverished southern Italy build a large, up-to-date hospital? The seeds of this great work were planted the evening of January 9, 1940, when Pio and three of his friends chatted in his monastery cell at Our Lady of Grace in San Giovanni.

Pio and his friends were discussing common problems—physical, emotional, and spiritual—that touch all our lives. From this heavy topic, Pio suddenly switched to the brighter and more consoling subjects of God's love for his people and their love for God. "Love is the spark of God in a man's soul; it is the very essence of God personified in the Holy Spirit," he said. "To God we owe all our love, which, to be adequate, ought to be infinite. But this cannot be, because God alone is infinite. We must at least give our whole being to love, to charity."[2]

As Padre Pio continued to talk about God's love, he convinced his three friends to join him in making his vision of building a modern hospital a reality. Many insisted that an up-to-date hospital on San Giovanni's rocky, barren mountainside—which rose approximately twenty-four hundred feet above sea level—could not be built. Others scoffed at the difficulty of securing building supplies for the project site when Foggia, the nearest sizable town, was twenty-five miles away, along rough roads. But Padre Pio was confident. He knew that if God wanted a modern hospital built in San Giovanni to minister to the sick, then God would clear all the obstacles that lay ahead. Pio's confidence was well placed. On May 5, 1956, when the hospital opened, Padre Pio was there to inaugurate it.

Padre Pio also reached out in love to heal the sick—sometimes with miraculous results. After many years of waging a private war against Pio and the Christian faith, San Giovanni's Dr. Francesco Riccardi lay dying of stomach cancer. He was loved by the villagers, because for years he had freely treated those who could not afford to pay. Although the physician was an atheist, the peasants from the surrounding area, as an act of love and faith, gathered together in the heavy sleet and howling winter winds outside his window and prayed for him. While they asked God to inspire Dr. Riccardi to believe in God and make his peace with him, the local priest went in to see him.

"I don't want any priests!" the doctor screamed. "Leave me in peace! Only Padre Pio could confess me. But I have offended him too much for him to come. . . . Therefore, I will die as I have lived."

Padre Pio was summoned, and he hurried to the doctor's bedside. As Pio opened his arms with a wide gesture and smiled, the doctor responded with amazement and asked for God's forgiveness. He made his confession and received the Sacrament of the Sick. But instead of dying, he completely recovered. In just three days, the cancer, which had been ready to claim his life, disappeared.[3]

In addition to the stigmata and the gift of healing, Pio possessed a multitude of other spiritual gifts, including prophecy and bilocation, which is the ability to appear at two different locations at the same time. But spiritual gifts do not necessarily indicate a person's holiness. Pio knew that only God, who is love, could make him holy and loving. As St. Paul wrote, "If I have prophetic powers, and understand all mysteries and all knowledge . . . but do not have love, I am nothing" (1 Corinthians 13:2).

Pause: Reflect on how God has manifested his love for you this week. How have you loved him in return by loving and serving others?

PIO'S WORDS

The pivot of perfection is love. He who lives in love lives in God, because "God is love," as the apostle says [1 John 4:8]. . . . Try always to advance in charity; enlarge your heart with confidence for the divine gifts which the Holy Spirit is anxious to pour into it. God can reject everything in a creature conceived in sin. . . . But God can absolutely not reject the sincere desire to love him. . . . If in a soul there is nothing else but the longing to love its God, everything else is there already because God is not present where there is no desire to love him. Say to God, "Do you want greater love from me? I have no more. Give me more, therefore, and I will offer it to you." Do not doubt; God will accept this offer. . . . Love is the queen of virtues. As the pearls are held together by the thread, thus the virtues are held together by love; and as the pearls fall when the thread breaks, thus the virtues are lost if love diminishes.[4]

Rising above selfishness, we must bow down to the sufferings and wounds of our fellow humans. We must make them our own, knowing how to suffer with our brethren for the love of God. We must know how to instill hope into their hearts and bring back a smile to their lips, having restored a ray of light into their souls. Then we shall be offering God the most beautiful, the most noble of prayers because our prayer will have sprung from sacrifice. It will be the very essence of love, the unselfish gift of all that we are in body and soul. In every sick individual there is Jesus suffering . . . in every person who is both sick and poor, Jesus is doubly visible.[5]

REFLECTION

In his deep love for God and for humanity, Padre Pio viewed everyone as children of God. He loved even those who were great sinners, and he advised his penitents never to doubt God's love for them, even if they should sin. Above all, he urged them to obey the commandment of love: "The LORD is our God, the LORD alone. You shall love the LORD your God with all your heart, and with all your soul, and with all your might" (Deuteronomy 6:4-5).

᠅ Think of a time when the weight of your sins kept you from turning to God and asking for forgiveness because you doubted his love for you. What made you realize that God loved you so much that he longed to forgive and bless you? Meditate on the following words spoken by Jesus: "A certain creditor had two debtors; one owed five hundred denarii, and the other fifty. When they could not pay, he canceled the debts for both of them. Now which of them will love him more?" (Luke 7:41-42) If you still doubt God's desire to love and forgive you, ask him to help you experience his love so that you will never doubt it in the future.

᠅ Do you know anyone who claims to have a great love for God and yet does not hesitate to break one or more of God's commandments? Examine your conscience and recall when you, too, claimed to love God and yet broke his laws. "They who have my commandments and keep them are those who love me" (John 14:21). Ask God for the grace to remain obedient to him in all things and in that way, to love him more and more each day.

☙ Consider Pio's words: "Although Jesus is pleased with you, he wishes you to grow more and more in love by perfecting your own soul, by bringing new souls to him all the time, and also by leading on to perfection those souls who are already in his sanctifying grace."[6] How might you apply Pio's advice to people in your life, such as family members, friends, and acquaintances?

☙ Padre Pio said, "The most certain proof of love is to suffer for the one we love, and since the Son of God suffered so much for pure love, there can no longer be any doubt that the cross carried for him becomes lovable in proportion to our love."[7]

Gaze on a crucifix and meditate on how Christ's love for us led him to willingly suffer and die for us. Think of someone you love, perhaps your children, and the sacrifices you have made for them because you loved them. Then think of someone who loved you in a sacrificial way. How did these sacrifices help your love to grow for that person? Ask the Lord to show you ways this week that you can love those who are close to you in a sacrificial way.

GOD'S WORD

We love [God] because he first loved us. (1 John 4:19)

Closing Prayer: Father, shower me with your love each day. I need your love in my heart to be the source for my love. May I grow each day in my love for you, and may I manifest that love by loving all the people in my life through my words, actions, and prayers.

1. Frederico Abresch, *The Voice of Padre Pio* (San Giovanni Rotondo, Italy: Rewarded Printing Shop, 1954), p. 5.

2. Pascal P. Parente, *Padre Pio: A City on a Mountain* (Washington, New Jersey: Ave Maria Institute, n.d.), pp. 123–24.

3. Maria Winowska, *The True Face of Padre Pio* (London: Souvenir Press, 1955), pp. 140–41.

4. Abresch, *The Voice of Padre Pio*, pp. 5–9.

5. Parente, *Padre Pio: A City on a Mountain*, pp. 123–24.

6. Padre Pio, *Letters,* vol. 1, 2nd ed., ed. Gerardo Di Flumeri (San Giovanni Rotondo, Italy: Our Lady of Grace Capuchin Friary, 1984), p. 706.

7. Alessio Parente, *Our Lady of Grace Prayer Book* (San Giovanni Rotondo, Italy: Our Lady of Grace Capuchin Friary, 1988), p. 187.

Heavenly Obedience

Theme: "Where there is no obedience, there is no virtue," said Pio. "Where there is no virtue, there is no good. Where good is lacking, there is no love. Where there is no love, God is absent. Where God is absent, there is no heaven."[1]

Opening Prayer: Help me, Lord, to discern your will in all circumstances. Inspire and motivate me to always obey you, no matter what way you choose to speak to me—whether through prayer, Scripture, or a trusted friend.

ABOUT PIO

Padre Pio's holiness and spiritual gifts drew the attention of millions of souls from around the world. However, he and his fellow priests and monks never allowed their monastery to become a "shrine" for the hundreds of thousands of pilgrims who traveled to San Giovanni Rotondo. Along with his fellow monks and priests, Pio daily followed the normally prescribed religious routines. In all matters, he obeyed his superiors. In fact, even when it caused him great personal pain, Pio obeyed.

For a two-year period in the 1930s, the church forbade Pio to practice any of his priestly duties except to say Mass privately. Padre Pio called this difficult period, from June 1931 to July 1933, his "imprisonment," but he did not hesitate to obey. During his "imprisonment," Padre Pio did not complain about the unfairness of the restrictions placed on him, nor did he fight to vindicate himself or rebel by going against the decree of the pope. Instead, he humbly accepted everything as the will of God. Pio lifted up his sufferings to Jesus in atonement for the sins of the world and for the souls in purgatory.

Padre Pio did not find out what had caused the Vatican to issue the edict until July 14, 1933, when it was lifted. It was then that Vatican officials told Pio's superiors at the friary that the decree had been based on false accusations given to Pope Pius XI by a few well-known prelates.

In refusing to compromise on the issue of obedience, Pio showed authentic humility. For example, during the two-year ban, Padre Pio was not permitted to see visitors. A few months after the edict was issued, a Chicago physician decided to travel to Italy to study Pio's stigmata. He spent ten days on a ship to Italy and then thirty hours on a train in order to reach San Giovanni. When he arrived at the monastery and asked to see Padre Pio, the monks told him that Pio was forbidden to receive visitors. The doctor insisted, so the monks went to Pio and asked him for a personal message for the doctor. They returned with the following message: "I am sorry that you have had to make this long journey in vain, but you will find it easy to understand that a monk *has to obey*." According to one of Pio's biographers,

"This reply impressed [the American doctor] more profoundly than any examination of the stigmata would have done."[2]

As Pio knew, obedience often requires self-sacrifice, courage, and generosity. Just as Jesus took up his cross, we too are to take up our crosses each day and follow Jesus. Just as Jesus accepted his sorrows and suffering in obedience to his Father, so we can do the same—even in the minor aggravations and frustrations we encounter each day, such as when a rude driver cuts us off on the road or when our children forget to take off their dirty shoes in the house. Padre Pio advised, "Make a particular effort to practice sweetness and submission to the will of God, not only where extraordinary matters are concerned, but also in little daily events. . . . And if you should happen to fail in some way, humble yourself, make a new proposition, pick yourself up, and carry on."[3]

Pio's obedience to God was severely tested in 1918, months before he received the visible stigmata. From his childhood, evil spirits had battered him spiritually as well as physically, sometimes even throwing him out of bed. But this spiritual battle seemed to reach its zenith in the months before Pio's stigmata appeared. During those agonizing times that year, as he struggled to follow the Lord despite the spiritual battles he had to fight, he often cried out to his heavenly Father as Christ had done on the cross, "My God, my God, why have you forsaken me?" (Mark 15:34). But as Christ had done the moment before he died on the cross, Pio, in his spiritual agony, humbly said to God, "Father, into your hands I commend my spirit" (Luke 23:46). Pio knew that everything in his life, whether pleasant or painful, was permitted by God for his spiritual growth as well as for the good of others. So in humble obedience, Pio offered up to Jesus his "internal martyrdom" as a prayer for the salvation of sinners.

A June 4, 1918, letter to his superior, Fr. Benedetto Nardella of San Marco in Lamis, exemplifies Padre Pio's undying desire to obey God even during his spiritual battles: "Implore help for me from heaven to attain perfect conformity to God's divine and holy designs . . . and to attain resolute, constant, and unshaken docility where obedience is concerned, which is my one support in the raging storm, the only raft to which I can cling in this spiritual shipwreck."[4]

Padre Pio's sufferings, whether physical, spiritual, or emotional, helped him empathize with those who sought his advice. For example, in reply to a complaint from one of his followers that sometimes obedience meant she had to suffer, Pio wrote,

You must continue to obey despite the interior conflict. . . . Jesus' obedience in the Garden and on the cross was marked by immense conflict, and he knew no relief; but he obeyed . . . and his obedience was excellent and all the more beautiful because it was so painful. Your soul, therefore, has never been more acceptable to God as it is now that you are obeying in the midst of aridity.[5]

Thousands of people, including many who knew him personally, believed that the virtue that best characterized Pio was his humble, heroic obedience. Almost ten years after Pio's death, Fr. Alberto D'Apolito, a devoted friend, wrote, "At an advanced age, remembering his younger years, Pio prayed, 'I heard the voice to obey you, oh true and good God. I wanted to obey you . . . and I have always wanted to obey you. . . . You called me to a religious life, and I obeyed. . . . You made me a partner of Jesus in suffering, and I obeyed.'"[6]

Pope John Paul II also singled out Padre Pio's virtue of obedience, noting that he offers a witness of extraordinary fidelity. On May 3, 1999, the day after Pio's beatification, the pope said,

Francis was his baptismal name, and he was a worthy follower of [St. Francis of Assisi] in poverty, chastity, and obedience from the time he first entered the friary. He practiced the Capuchin rule in the entirety of its rigor, generously embracing the life of penance. He found no gratification in pain, but chose it as a way of expiation and purification. Like the Poor Man of Assisi, he aimed at conformity to Jesus Christ, desiring only "to love and to suffer," in order to help the Lord in the exhausting and demanding work of salvation. In "firm, constant, and iron" obedience, Pio found the highest expression of his unconditional love for God and the church.[7]

Pause: Reflect on Padre Pio's example of unquestioning obedience. What does this example mean for your own life?

PIO'S WORDS

"One day a woman said to Pio, 'I am ashamed to tell you this, but I believe I love you more than I love God.' 'Very well,' said Pio, 'then you will do as I say. I want you to go to the village and steal for me.' The shocked woman replied, 'Padre Pio, what are you saying? You know I can't do that.'

"Pio very sternly continued, 'I meant what I said; go to the village and steal for me.' The woman answered, 'No, no, Padre. I don't want to steal. It's wrong to steal.'

"After repeating the command to her for the third time, and the woman still insisting that it was wrong to steal, Pio smiled and said, 'Don't you see? When I commanded you to do something contrary to the law of God, you refused to obey me; therefore, you love God more than you love me.' Then he added, 'You love me because I lead you to God. If I did not lead you to God, you would no longer love me.'"[8]

REFLECTION

Why do we need to value obedience to God? Doesn't obedience take away our personal freedom? On the contrary, obedience to God actually sets us free to love him more deeply. When we sin, we show preference for our will over God's; we show that we love ourselves more than we love him. On the other hand, because God created us to know, love, serve, and obey him, we progress along the road to heaven when we choose to follow his will.

We must also try to be obedient to the quiet voice of the Holy Spirit, who may have something specific for us to do, such as reaching out to someone in love. For example, the Holy Spirit may be nudging us to call an old friend or acquaintance or to talk to a newcomer at Mass. When we are obedient to God's call, even when we must step out of our "comfort zone," we allow him to use us to extend his kingdom on earth.

How willing are you to obey God, even when he speaks to you through ordinary people in your life, such as your spouse, your parents, your pastor, or your spiritual director? What obstacles in yourself do you encounter in trying to be obedient to God's call in your life?

Whenever you struggle with your own personal issues of obedience, call to mind pertinent Scripture verses and allow the Holy

Spirit to enlighten, encourage, and strengthen you through them. One example: "'God opposes the proud, but gives grace to the humble.' Humble yourselves therefore under the mighty hand of God, so that he may exalt you in due time" (1 Peter 5:5-6). Other verses you could pray are Matthew 18:4 and 23:12 and James 4:6-10.

❧ One by one, meditate on the following scenes from Christ's life. As you do this, note which ones speak to you most powerfully about the obedience of Jesus, Mary, or Joseph.

- The unhesitating obedience of Mary when she said "yes" to bearing God's only begotten Son (see Luke 1:28-38).

- The obedience of Joseph and Mary in complying with Jewish customs when they presented the Christ Child to God in the Temple at Jerusalem (see Luke 2:22-24).

- Jesus' obedience to his mother at the wedding feast at Cana, where he changed water into wine (see John 2:1-11).

- Jesus' obedience to civil authority when he ordered Peter to pay the required taxes for both of them (see Matthew 22:21).

- The culmination of the obedience of Jesus in the Garden of Gethsemane when he foresaw his horrendous passion. To his Father he said, "If it is possible, let this cup pass from me; yet not what I want but what you want" (see Matthew 26:39).

GOD'S WORD

Let the same mind be in you that was in Christ Jesus, who, though he was in the form of God, did not regard equality with God as something to be exploited, but emptied himself, taking the form of a slave, being born in human likeness. And being found in human form, he humbled himself and became obedient to the point of death—even death on a cross. (Philippians 2:5-8)

Closing Prayer: Dear Jesus, you are the ultimate model of obedience. In the daily challenges that come my way, help me to obey your will, even when you ask me to do something difficult or uncomfortable. I know that you will give me the grace to do all that you call me to do. *Lord, I believe you will help me obey You; help my unbelief.*

1. Frederico Abresch, *The Voice of Padre Pio* (San Giovanni Rotondo, Italy: Rewarded Printing Shop, 1954), pp. 13–14.

2. Maria Winowska, *The True Face of Padre Pio* (London: Souvenir

Press, 1955), pp. 164–65.

3. Padre Pio, *Letters,* vol. 3, 2nd ed., ed. Gerardo Di Flumeri (San Giovanni Rotondo, Italy: Our Lady of Grace Capuchin Friary, 2001), pp. 939–40.

4. Padre Pio, *Letters,* vol. 1, 2nd ed., ed. Gerardo Di Flumeri (San Giovanni Rotondo, Italy: Our Lady of Grace Capuchin Friary, 1984), p. 1149.

5. Pio, *Letters,* vol. 3, p. 1020.

6. Alberto D'Apolito, *Padre Pio of Pietrelcina* (San Giovanni Rotondo, Italy: Our Lady of Grace Capuchin Friary, 1986), p. 261.

7. Gennaro Preziuso, *The Life of Padre Pio: Between the Altar and the Confessional* (New York: Alba House, 2000), p. 236.

8. Dorothy M. Gaudiose, *Padre Pio* (Westwood, NJ: Westwood Printing, n.d.), p. 10.

Jesus Suffers with You

Theme: "You are suffering, it is true," Pio said. "Fear not, because God is with you. . . . You suffer, but believe also that Jesus himself suffers in you and for you."[1]

Opening Prayer: Let us pray with St. Pio as he meditates on Christ's sufferings: "O Jesus, let nothing ever separate me from you. Let me cling to your sufferings, loving you to the utmost of my power. Grant that I may die with you on Calvary and so to ascend to you in glory . . . [where I will] love you face to face in heaven and sing your praise eternally."[2]

ABOUT PIO

Even during his early years, Padre Pio desired to identify with Christ's passion, so much so that he was drawn to physical mortification—practices that were more common and accepted during his lifetime than they are today. When his mother, Giuseppa, found out that he was regularly beating himself with a chain, she became deeply concerned. When Giuseppa asked him why he was beating himself, Pio told her that he "had to beat himself like the Jews had beaten Jesus."[3]

However, throughout his life, Pio was drawn to suffering not for its own sake but as a way to draw closer to Christ and to suffer for the good of humanity. Like St. Paul, he believed that "I am now rejoicing in my sufferings for your sake, and in my flesh I am completing what is lacking in Christ's afflictions for the sake of his body, that is, the church" (Colossians 1:24). Of course, Christ does not need our help to save souls. His suffering alone redeemed humanity. But God grants us the privilege of offering up our own sufferings along with Christ's on the cross. Padre Pio believed that our suffering has meaning and value in a world broken by sin. In his many ecstasies, he would often offer himself as a "victim to the Lord for poor sinners."[4]

Padre Pio took every opportunity to suffer along with Christ, especially when he celebrated the Sacrifice of the Mass. Alluding to his preparations for his daily Mass, Pio said, "Only Jesus can understand what I suffer, as I prepare for the sorrowful scene of Calvary."[5] According to Fr. Aurelio Laita, the former vicar general of the Capuchin Friars' order, Padre Pio "made the Eucharist not only the center of his life, but also the moment of his daily sacrifice, moved by his wish to take part in the sufferings of Christ for the good of mankind."[6]

Padre Pio knew that the cross of Christ was central to our understanding of God's love and forgiveness. As we embrace the crosses in our own life, we grow in our love for Jesus as we begin to comprehend the great sacrifice he made for us. This understanding also gives us the strength to suffer for Christ. Pio advised, "Reflect yourself in Jesus in agony on the cross for our sake, and you, too, shall find the strength to suffer for his sake."[7] Padre Pio certainly knew this truth from his own experience, as he found the strength to endure the suffering of the visible stigmata, the bleeding wounds of Christ, for fifty years, from 1918 until his death in 1968. He understood that we cannot experience the glory of the resurrection without experiencing the cross of Calvary.

In a September 16, 1916, letter to one of his spiritual children, Pio recommended that in the midst of trials and suffering, the soul should meditate on Jesus:

> The soul should habitually meditate on the life, passion, and death of our Lord Jesus. . . . It is true that, given our condition, it is not within our power to keep our thoughts always fixed on God, but let us do our best to keep ourselves, as far as possible, in his presence. This we can and must do, calling to mind every now and then the great truth that God sees us. . . .
>
> Don't worry if the trials increase, because it is written that souls who move closest to God must be more greatly tried [see Sirach 2:1]. May the most consoling thought that the heavenly Father deemed you worthy, in this also, to be made similar to his most beloved Son, urge you to suffer in a resigned manner. Courage, therefore and go forward always. . . . You will obtain the prize reserved for strong souls.[8]

While we are experiencing pain and trials we may still wonder why we should offer our sufferings to God. As one of Pio's biographers explained, "We are playing for high stakes, the highest possible, to save souls, as Padre Pio did by his redemptive suffering."[9] If we try to follow Pio's example of enduring patiently and willingly whatever sufferings come our way, we will be sharing in this work of saving souls. Pio said, "Souls have to be bought."[10] Having this truth firmly implanted in our hearts can help us to see value in our adverse circumstances and to endure them with joy—just as Padre Pio did.

Pause: Think of a time in your life when you were suffering. How did Jesus suffer "in you and for you"?

PIO'S WORDS

The Lord burdens us and sets us free from our burdens, for when he bestows a cross on one of his chosen ones, he strengthens that soul to such an extent that by bearing the weight of this cross [the soul] is relieved of it. . . . Like the Virgin, remain at the cross of Jesus, and you will never be deprived of comfort.[11]

When one of his spiritual children complained to Pio about her intense suffering, he replied,
   I cannot but admire and bless our heavenly Father for

such exquisite behavior of his divine love towards you. How can I not rejoice at the sight of so many trials to which the good Lord is subjecting you? Isn't the cross the certain and infallible proof of God's great love for a soul?

I could not be pleased with you if I did not see you so tested. So take heart; bless the hand that afflicts you for the sole purpose of sanctifying you and rendering you similar to his only begotten Son. Don't believe that the Lord is irritated with you and therefore subjects you to such harsh trials. You would be greatly mistaken in this. The Lord wants to test your fidelity; to inebriate you with the cross of his Son; to purify you; and to increase your [eternal reward].

Remember and keep well impressed in your mind that Calvary is the hill of the saints, but remember also that after having climbed Calvary, the cross having been erected and you having died on it, you will immediately ascend another mount, called Tabor, the heavenly Jerusalem. Remember that the suffering is short lived but the reward is eternal." [12]

REFLECTION

Suffering will always remain a mystery, but we can, like Padre Pio, embrace suffering and use it for our good and the good of others. Do you believe, as Sts. Paul and Pio did, that we are called to share in Christ's redeeming work? God really will accept and use your freely offered sufferings in reparation for sinners and for their salvation. Do you believe that God can help you grow closer to him through suffering? God can forge your character through suffering and help you become more compassionate. Do you believe that he will strengthen you by his grace as you suffer? God will not abandon you in your suffering; he will be with you always (see Mathew 28:20).

❧ We have a choice. We can look back at our lives and dwell on the troubles and heartaches others have caused us. We can declare that our parents did not raise us correctly or that they caused us misery. We can blame our failures, weaknesses, and flaws on others in our past. But does that do us any good *now*? Consider that everything that has happened to you in the past—the bad as well as the good—contributed to your arrival at this point in your life, in which you seek God and greater holiness, in which you love Jesus and seek to love him more. If you could eliminate from your past anything or anyone on whom you blame your failings, perhaps you would not have arrived at this point.

Examine how God has been speaking to you in your past and present sufferings. Visualize each occasion and imagine the crucified Christ present in each of those situations. After this reflection, inhale deeply, mentally letting go of the painful memories. Then acknowledge, accept, and thank God for his faithful presence in your life during the bad times as well as the good.

✿ When you or your family or friends are suffering, meditate on Colossians 1:24: "I am now rejoicing in my sufferings for your sake, and in my flesh I am completing what is lacking in Christ's afflictions for the sake of his body, that is, the church." Or, hum or sing—aloud or silently—"Amazing Grace," especially the verse that says, "Through many dangers, toils, and snares, I have already come. 'Tis grace hath brought me safe thus far, and grace will lead me home."[13]

✿ Recall a recent time when God allowed you to suffer. How did that experience of suffering enable you to grow spiritually? Share your story with a family member or close friend.

GOD'S WORD

When we cry, "Abba! Father!" it is that very Spirit bearing witness with our spirit that we are children of God, and if children, then heirs, heirs of God and joint heirs with Christ—if, in fact, we suffer with him so that we may also be glorified with him. I consider that the sufferings of this present time are not worth comparing with the glory about to be revealed to us. (Romans 8:15-18)

Closing Prayer: O suffering Jesus, forgive me for not accepting the miseries of my past. When each occurred, I could have offered each to you for the salvation of others and myself. From this time forward, Lord, give me the grace to accept my sufferings, to unite them to yours, and to thereby participate in your redeeming work.

1. Frederico Abresch, *The Voice of Padre Pio* (San Giovanni Rotondo, Italy: Rewarded Printing Shop, 1954), p. 33.

2. Nesta De Robeck, *Padre Pio* (Milwaukee: The Bruce Publishing Company, 1958), p. 124.

3. Gennaro Preziuso, "The Parents of Padre Pio," in *The Voice of Padre Pio*, vol. 35, ed. Capuchin Friars (San Giovanni Rotondo, Italy: Capuchin Friars, Nov.–Dec., 2005), pp. 10–11.

4. Padre Pio, *Letters,* vol. 1, 2nd ed., ed. Gerardo Di Flumeri (San Giovanni Rotondo, Italy: Our Lady of Grace Capuchin Friary, 1984), p. 756.

5. Alessio Parente, *Our Lady of Grace Prayer Book* (San Giovanni Rotondo, Italy: Our Lady of Grace Capuchin Friary, 1988), p. 203.

6. Luigi Gravina, "The Vigil of Saint Pio," in *The Voice of Padre Pio*, vol. 35, ed. Capuchin Friars (San Giovanni Rotondo, Italy: Capuchin Friars, Nov.–Dec., 2005), p. 20.

7. Nello Castello, *Padre Pio Teaches Us* (Bari, Italy: Favia Printers, 1981), p. 237.

8. Padre Pio, *Letters,* vol. 3, 2nd ed., ed. Gerardo Di Flumeri (San Giovanni Rotondo, Italy: Our Lady of Grace Capuchin Friary, 2001), pp. 255–58.

9. Stella Lilley, *On the Road with Padre Pio* (San Giovanni Rotondo, Italy: Edizioni Padre Pio da Pietrelcina, n.d.), p. 245.

10. Lilley, *On the Road with Padre Pio*, p. 245.

11. Parente, *Our Lady of Grace Prayer Book*, pp. 53–54.

12. Pio, *Letters,* vol. 3, pp. 252–53.

13. John Newton, "Amazing Grace," in *Charles Johnson's One Hundred & One Famous Hymns,* ed. Mary Ann Thorson (Delavan, WI: Hallberg Publishing Corporation, 1983), p. 49.

Jesus in the Eucharist

Theme: "Padre Pio felt drawn by a mysterious force before being united with Jesus in the Eucharist. He counted the hours separating him from the beginning of his Mass."[1]

Opening Prayer: Let us pray with Pio, as he recalled his reception of Jesus in the Blessed Sacrament: "Jesus, my food! . . . Yes, Jesus, I love you; at this moment it seems to me that I love you and I also feel the need to love you more. But, Jesus, I have no more love left in my heart. You know that I have given it all to you. If you want more love, take this heart of mine and fill it with your love, then command me to love and I shall not refuse. I beg you to do this; I desire it."[2]

ABOUT PIO

Padre Pio's parents, Orazio and Giuseppa Forgione, instilled in him a great devotion to Christ in the Eucharist. As a child growing up in Pietrelcina, young Francesco visited the local church twice a day to offer his love to Christ in the tabernacle. He enjoyed his role as altar server because it allowed him to remain near the priest as he consecrated the host. Francesco longed to be a priest so that he, too, could be God's instrument in changing the bread and wine into the body and blood of Jesus Christ.

Once he was ordained, many who witnessed Padre Pio celebrating the Mass noted that he seemed to embody the reality of what was actually happening at the altar. As our faith teaches us, the Mass makes present the paschal sacrifice (see *Catechism of the Catholic Church*, 1364). Writing more than ten years before Pio's death, author Malachy Carroll described, from personal experience, how Padre Pio celebrated the Mass:

Perhaps it is safe to say that nowhere in our world is there another priest who celebrates Mass as though he were bearing his cross through every moment of it. He indeed bears witness to the passion of Christ in his own body. There is an expression of suffering on his face at the supreme moments of the Mass, and his body is sometimes seen to twitch with pain. His fingers tremble and hesitate about breaking the Host, as though the veil has been rent for him and the reality of what he is doing has become too intense. His lips shiver as he raises the Chalice to them. When he genuflects, it is as though an invisible cross has crushed him down, for he rises painfully and with the utmost difficulty. There are moments when he seems lost in colloquy with God. . . . Sometimes he weeps, as though a shadow of the world's sin has come between him and the Host, and his compassion is great for the Christ he sees mocked again. And there are those hands exposed only in the Mass, and otherwise hidden by the brown woolen mittens he constantly wears. Those hands can be seen with the bloody marks on them, the mystic shadow of the nails. And sometimes they bleed.

Behind the wonder that is Padre Pio, there is a divine purpose, and that purpose may well find its supreme expression in the Mass of Padre Pio.[3]

Fr. Alessio Parente, Pio's fellow Capuchin, friend, and caretaker, who attended hundreds of the Masses Pio celebrated, made these observations:

[Pio] remained a long time as if unable to move, his eyes full of tears and invariably fixed on the crucifix, while he offered to the heavenly Father the bread and wine that were to become the body and blood of Jesus. When Pio raised the paten and chalice, his sleeves fell back a little and revealed the wounds in his hands on which the eyes of all those present rested with deep emotion. But the culminating point of his Mass was the consecration. With sobs and tears . . . the stigmatized priest reenacted the divine tragedy of Calvary to the point of showing forth in his own pierced flesh the awful torment of Jesus crucified.[4]

At the consecration, said Fr. Parente, Padre Pio placed "his lips near the Host which he held between his fingers, [and] with infinite tenderness he exclaimed, 'Jesus, my Food!'"[5] Even after Communion, Fr. Parente noted, "instead of being satisfied, [Pio's] hunger and thirst for Jesus in the Eucharist increased. His heartbeats had an accelerated rhythm. He felt as though . . . he burned with a divine flame. In the choir afterwards, he was immersed in an intimate, silent prayer of Eucharistic thanksgiving and praise."[6]

Sometimes, although we desire to receive the Eucharist, we feel unworthy. "This is true; we're not worthy of such a gift," Padre Pio acknowledged, but explained, "It is one thing to take it unworthily because of mortal sin, and another to *be* unworthy. We are all unworthy, but he himself invites us. . . . Let us be humble and receive him with a loving heart."[7] Gennaro Preziuso, an Italian journalist and author, said, "Padre Pio considered the Holy Eucharist as 'the great means for aspiring to perfection.' He wanted his spiritual sons and daughters to approach the altar daily with faith and love, to receive 'the Bread of Angels.'"[8]

Pause: How is Jesus present to you when you receive him in the Eucharist?

PIO'S WORDS

During the course of the day, when you are unable to do anything else, call on Jesus even in the midst of all your occupations, with resigned groanings of the soul. He will come to stay united to your soul always, through his grace and holy love. Fly in spirit before the tabernacle when you cannot go there with the body, and there express your ardent desires. Speak to, pray to, and embrace the Beloved of souls, better than if you had been able to receive him sacramentally.[9]

Let us approach to receive the Bread of Angels with great faith and with a great flame of love in our hearts. Let us await this most tender Lover of our souls in order to be consoled in this life with the kiss of his mouth.[10]

Let us humble ourselves profoundly and confess that if God were not our breastplate and shield, we should at once be pierced by every kind of sin. This is why we must invariably keep ourselves in God by persevering in our spiritual exercises. On the other hand, we must always have courage, and if some spiritual languor comes upon us, let us run to the feet of Jesus in the Blessed Sacrament and let us place ourselves in the midst of the heavenly perfumes and we will undoubtedly regain our strength.[11]

REFLECTION

Why did Padre Pio love the Eucharist so much? In addition to parents who inspired in him Eucharistic devotion, Pio had frequent contact throughout his childhood with holy priests and religious people. Starting when he was five years old until his death in 1968, Pio had visions of Jesus, Mary, and his guardian angel. These experiences convinced him that what the church taught about the real presence of Christ in the Eucharist was true. Padre Pio also believed Jesus' words in Scripture that he was the "living bread that came down from heaven" and that if we eat this bread we will "live forever" (John 6:51).

However, one of the greatest influences on Pio's devotion to the Eucharist was that he witnessed a transformation in people when they began to receive the Blessed Sacrament, either for the first time or for the first time after having neglected the sacraments for many years.

How might you grow in your own love for the Blessed Sacrament? Simply spend more time before the tabernacle, allowing Jesus' love to touch your heart and soul. You could also study Scripture passages that directly speak about the Eucharist, such as Jesus' words in John 6:30-58. Remember, too, that faith is a gift (see Ephesians 2:8-9), so do not hesitate to ask Jesus for the gift of believing in his real presence in the Eucharist.

As you grow in your love of Christ in the Blessed Sacrament, recall Padre Pio's deep devotion to the Eucharist. Allow his example to help you open up more fully to Jesus' real presence.

❧ Do you, like Pio, hunger for the Eucharist? When circumstances prevent you from going to church and receiving Jesus in the Blessed Sacrament, Padre Pio would assure you that you can—no matter where you are physically—visit God in the tabernacle and receive Christ's body and blood spiritually. Consider the following methods Pio employed to either physically or spiritually "rest" in Jesus' presence in the Eucharist:

- "Run to the feet of Jesus in the Blessed Sacrament" and place yourself "in the midst of the heavenly perfumes" and you will "undoubtedly regain strength."

- No matter where you are, you can turn your inner "gaze toward the tabernacle."

- "Fly in spirit before the tabernacle when you cannot go there with the body, and there express your ardent desires. Speak to, pray to, and embrace the Beloved of souls, better than if you had been able to receive him sacramentally."

Relax, close your eyes, and imagine yourself before the tabernacle. Breathe deeply, exhale slowly, and feel your whole body relaxing before God's loving presence. Meditate on Christ in the Eucharist, and as you do, dialogue with Jesus dwelling in the tabernacle. You can use one of the following Scripture passages to help guide your meditation and dialogue:

- "He rained down on them manna to eat, and gave them the grain of heaven. Mortals ate of the bread of angels." (Psalm 78:24-25).

- In perfect trust we can go to Jesus who loves us and who said, "Come to me" (Matthew 11:28).

- Jesus said, "I am the way, and the truth, and the life" (John 14:6). If we focus on Christ, we will *find* that way, that truth, and that life.

✛ Create a litany that praises Jesus in the Eucharist, or use the litany in the closing prayer below. As you pray the litany, place yourself in a relaxed sitting or reclining position, and, with deep and slow breathing, lift up your heart and soul to Jesus.

GOD'S WORD

[Jesus said,] "I am the bread of life. Your ancestors ate the manna in the wilderness, and they died. This is the bread that comes down from heaven, so that one may eat of it and not die. I am the living bread that came down from heaven. Whoever eats of this bread will live forever; and the bread that I will give for the life of the world is my flesh. . . .

"Very truly, I tell you, unless you eat the flesh of the Son of Man and drink his blood, you have no life in you. Those who eat my flesh and drink my blood have eternal life, and I will raise them up on the last day; for my flesh is true food and my blood is true drink. Those who eat my flesh and drink my blood abide in me, and I in them. Just as the living Father sent me, and I live because of the Father, so whoever eats me will live because of me. This is the bread that came down from heaven, not like that which your ancestors ate, and they died. But the one who eats this bread will live forever." (John 6:48-51, 53-58)

Closing Prayer:

Dear Jesus,

Fullness of grace and holy love . . . have mercy on us.

Bread of angels . . . have mercy on us.

Lover of my soul . . . have mercy on us.

Perennial sacrifice . . . have mercy on us.

Fruit of the Virgin's womb . . . have mercy on us.

Incarnation of the Word . . . have mercy on us.

The Way, the Truth, and the Life . . . have mercy on us.

Divine intimacy . . . have mercy on us.

My breastplate and shield . . . have mercy on us.

Beloved of my soul . . . have mercy on us.

Jesus my food . . . have mercy on us.

Sacrifice of love . . . have mercy on us.

Jesus, save your people.

1. Alessio Parente, *Padre Pio's Prayer Life* (San Giovanni Rotondo, Italy: Our Lady of Grace Capuchin Friary, 1994), p. 21.

2. Padre Pio, *Letters,* vol. 1, 2nd ed., ed. Gerardo Di Flumeri (San Giovanni Rotondo, Italy: Our Lady of Grace Capuchin Friary, 1984), pp. 299–300.

3. Malachy Carroll, *Padre Pio* (Dublin, Ireland: Cahill and Co. Limited, 1961), pp. 50–52.

4. Mary Ingoldsby, *Padre Pio: His Life and Mission* (Dublin, Ireland: Veritas Publications, 1978), p. 103.

5. Parente, *Padre Pio's Prayer Life,* p. 21.

6. Parente, *Padre Pio's Prayer Life,* p. 21.

7. Nello Castello, *Padre Pio Teaches Us* (Bari, Italy: Favia Printers, 981), p. 75.

8. Gennaro Preziuso, *The Life of Padre Pio: Between the Altar and the Confessional* (New York: Alba House, 2000), p. 184.

9. Padre Pio, *Letters,* vol. 3, 2nd ed., ed. Gerardo Di Flumeri (San Giovanni Rotondo, Italy: Our Lady of Grace Capuchin Friary, 2001), p. 452.

10. Padre Pio, *Letters,* vol. 2, 3rd ed., ed. Gerardo Di Flumeri (San Giovanni Rotondo, Italy: Our Lady of Grace Capuchin Friary, 2002), p. 508.

11. Padre Pio, *Letters,* vol. 3, p. 507.

MEDITATION EIGHT

The Passion of Jesus, No Greater Love

Theme: In his agony in the Garden of Gethsemane, Jesus foresaw all that he would have to endure. His inner pain was so great that he prayed, "My Father, if it is possible, let this cup pass from me; yet not what I want but what you want" (Matthew 26:39). In the passion of Jesus, we can see just how much he loves us. He accepted his suffering and death on the cross for love of each of us.

Opening Prayer: Let us pray with Pio: "O divine Spirit, enlighten and inflame me in meditating on the passion of Jesus, the Eternal and Immortal [One] who debased himself to undergo an immense martyrdom . . . in order to save the creature which has offended him."[1]

ABOUT PIO

By focusing on the wounds inflicted on Jesus during his scourging, crowning with thorns, carrying of the cross, and crucifixion, Pio sought to identify as fully as possible with his Savior. Meditating as often as possible on Christ's anguish during his passion, Pio offered his sufferings to Jesus in the hope of alleviating the pain our Lord suffers when people sin. Pio asked Jesus to give him as much suffering as God thought he could bear.

In 1911, Padre Pio took another step in faith by offering himself to Jesus as a "victim" for sinners, as well as for the souls in purgatory. God must have accepted Pio's offer, because on September 20, 1918, as Pio meditated alone before the crucifix in the friary loft, a mysterious being whose hands, feet, and side dripped with blood hovered in front of the priest. (In later years, Pio identified the being as Christ, crucified.)[2] Moments later, the being disappeared, and Pio discovered that his own hands, feet, and side were dripping with blood. Padre Pio's wounds bled continuously for the next fifty years, until just before his death.

Not only did Pio suffer the physical pain from his bleeding stigmata, he also endured the painful embarrassment of all the attention it attracted around the world. This humble priest, who wanted nothing more than to serve God and neighbor in the seclusion of the Capuchin friary in San Giovanni, suddenly faced the daily prying of the secular media and of brazen curiosity seekers. All of this probably caused Pio greater pain than did his bleeding wounds. But, as always, he accepted every kind of suffering God sent him and offered it up for the sake of sinners.

If, during Padre Pio's lifetime, you had attended one of the Masses he celebrated, you would have witnessed the complete immersion of his body, soul, and mind in the sacramental reenactment of Christ's last supper and passion. Almost ten years before Pio's death, Nesta de Robeck, who knew him well, wrote this witness of Pio as he celebrated Mass:

> Just as in his meditation, Padre Pio relives our Lord's agony in the Garden, so now [in his Mass], to an enhanced degree, he relives the passion and death of Christ; tears course down his cheeks and his face is that of suffering itself. The living sacrifice of Christ is being offered by a living person [Pio], bearing the marks of the cross [the stigmata] on his own body, who stands there in the place of the living Christ. The barriers between God and man fall, the way is opened, the light streams in, and the peace of God, made possible by the sacrifice of Calvary, is present among people.[3]

We show our true devotion to Christ by imitating him. "But in order to imitate him," wrote Pio, "we must reflect each day on the life of the One we intend to take as our model. From reflection is born esteem for his acts, and from esteem springs the desire and consolation of imitation."[4] Padre Pio's desire to imitate Christ was so powerful that he offered to suffer the passion with him. In an excerpt from a letter to his spiritual director, Fr. Agostino, Pio wrote, "It is incomprehensible how Jesus can be consoled not merely by those who sympathize with his torments, but when he finds a soul who for love of him asks not for consolations and only wants to be allowed to share in his sufferings."[5]

Today, Padre Pio continues to repeat to us, "Let us love Jesus in the passion more than anything else. Let us often meditate on the suffering of the God-Man."[6]

Pause: Why does Pio recommend reflection on the life of Jesus, and in particular, his passion?

PIO'S WORDS

Man savors sin, and on account of sin God is deathly sad; the pangs of a cruel agony make him sweat blood. . . . What depths of love does his heart not contain? His holy face is filled with sadness and utter tenderness. . . . O Jesus, my heart is overwhelmed when I think of the love which made you speed toward your passion. You have taught us that there is no greater love than to give one's life for those one loves. . . .

O my Jesus, give me strength when my weak nature rebels against all the ills that threaten it, so that I may with love accept the pain and distress of this life in exile. . . .

Destroy in me all that displeases you and imprint on my heart with the fire of your sacred love all your sufferings. . . . May my soul be intoxicated by your blood and be nourished by the bread of your suffering.[7]

With my whole strength I cling to your merits, your sufferings, your expiation, your tears, so that I may be able to cooperate with you in the work of salvation. Give me strength to fly from sin, the only cause of your agony, of your bloody sweat, and of your death.[8]

REFLECTION

Jesus entered the world to do the Father's loving will, which was to suffer and die in order to save us from our sins and give us eternal life (see John 6:38-40). If this is not a sign of God's love for us, what is? In his great desire for us to be united to him for all eternity, God the Father gave us his only begotten Son, who through his agonizing passion, atoned for all the sins of humanity.

Once we have accepted Christ's sacrifice for us, once we have turned from sin and begun to follow him, then who—now or ever—could separate us from God's love? (see 1 John 4:8) According to St. Paul, nothing can: "For I am convinced that neither death, nor life, nor angels, nor rulers, nor things present, nor things to come, nor powers, nor height, nor depth, nor anything else in all creation, will be able to separate us from the love of God in Christ Jesus our Lord" (Romans 8:38-39).

❧ Using your imagination, place yourself beside Christ's mother as she gazes on her dying Son (see John 19:25-27). As you envision this scene, reflect on the following:

- On the cross, Christ's blood flowed from hundreds of wounds. Consider the fact that Jesus would have suffered and died for you even if you were the only person on earth.

- Did the mother of Christ empathize so much with her son that she suffered along with him, feeling his every pain and humiliation? Now, kneeling beside her, do you also feel Christ's pain?

  Write in a prayer journal how you feel. What does Christ say to you about the suffering he endured? Ask him to let you experience the great love he had for you as he suffered to redeem you.

🙠 Spend some time reflecting on the questions below. You might want to write down the thoughts that come to you:

- How would I benefit spiritually from meditating on Christ's passion each day?

- How do I feel about Jesus' declaration that "no one has greater love than this, to lay down one's life for one's friends" (John 15:13)?

- How willing am I to "lay down" my own life for those I love by serving them, helping them, and listening to them, even when it inconveniences me?

Once you have finished your reflection, spend a few moments thanking Jesus for having laid down his life to save you.

✌ Commit to praying regularly for someone you know, perhaps even someone in your family, who has not yet come to know and accept God's love for her or him. Ask the Holy Spirit to help that person come to believe that Christ's passion, death, and resurrection manifest God's unfathomable love for him or her.

GOD'S WORD

Surely he has borne our infirmities
   and carried our diseases;
yet we accounted him stricken,
   struck down by God, and afflicted.
But he was wounded for our transgressions,
   crushed for our iniquities;
upon him was the punishment
      that made us whole,
   and by his bruises we are healed.
All we like sheep have gone astray;
   we have all turned to our own way,
and the LORD has laid on him
   the iniquity of us all.
(Isaiah 53:4-6)

Closing Prayer: Allow Pio's prayer to become your own: "O blood of Christ, thou art the irrefutable proof of the love which alone caused thee to flow. Let me be purified in thee. . . . O Jesus, let nothing ever separate me from thee."[9]

1. Nesta De Robeck, *Padre Pio* (Milwaukee: The Bruce Publishing Company, 1958), p. 115.

2. C. Bernard Ruffin, *Padre Pio: The True Story, Revised and Expanded* (Huntington, IN: Our Sunday Visitor Publishing Division, Our Sunday Visitor, Inc., 1991), p. 155.

3. De Robeck, *Padre Pio*, p. 59.

4. Padre Pio, *Letters*, vol. 1, 2nd ed., ed. Gerardo Di Flumeri (San Giovanni Rotondo, Italy: Our Lady of Grace Capuchin Friary, 1984), p. 1116.

5. Pio, *Letters*, vol. 1, p. 377.

6. Padre Pio, *Letters*, vol. 3, 2nd ed., ed. Gerardo Di Flumeri (San Giovanni Rotondo, Italy: Our Lady of Grace Capuchin Friary, 2001), p. 69.

7. Maria Winowska, *The True Face of Padre Pio* (London: Souvenir Press, 1955), pp. 168–69, 179.

8. De Robeck, *Padre Pio*, pp. 125–26.

9. De Robeck, *Padre Pio*, pp. 123–25.

True Holiness

Theme: We do not need special supernatural gifts to become holy. According to Padre Pio, "Holiness means . . . perfect mastery of all our passions. It means . . . preferring poverty rather than wealth, humiliation rather than glory, suffering rather than pleasure. Holiness means loving our neighbor as ourselves for love of God. . . . It means living humbly . . . and carrying out one's duties for no other reason than that of pleasing God."[1]

Opening Prayer: Holy Trinity, help me to master my passions, live humbly, and carry out my duties for your glory. Above all, enable me to love you and to love my neighbor.

ABOUT PIO

When we encounter holy people like Padre Pio, we often wonder what they were like as children. Were they always inclined towards God, or did they have a sudden conversion that changed the direction of their life? It seems that as a child, Pio was a good, obedient, but ordinary boy living in poverty, much like the young Jesus. Popular author and speaker Fr. Andrew Apostoli, CFR, said,

In Padre Pio's case, we have someone in whom the Holy Spirit formed a veritable living image of Jesus. . . . Like many a young boy from a little southern Italian town like Pietrelcina, young Francesco, the future saint, was born of typically poor, hardworking, God-fearing peasant parents. When asked in later life what he was like as a youth, Pio remarked that he was like *un macerone senza sale,* "a piece of spaghetti without any salt on it," a humorous way of saying his childhood was bland and uneventful.[2]

We often fail to perceive holiness in the ordinary, and we can be tempted to believe that Padre Pio's holiness was due to his amazing supernatural gifts. However, Fr. Alessio Parente, who cared for Pio during the saint's last years, knew that Pio's example of allowing himself to be consumed by the love of God and of neighbor was truly the basis of his holiness. Fr. Parente explained,

This [love] is the mark of holiness . . . the sign of a true Christian; the mark of one who follows the commandments of Jesus who said, "You shall love the Lord your God with all your heart, and with all your soul, and with all your mind. . . . You shall love your neighbor as yourself" (Matthew 22:37-39). Padre Pio's whole life was devoted to God and his neighbor. This is the mark of holiness, the true sign of sanctity. Perhaps we . . . are inclined to stand in awe, looking at his stigmata, his bilocation. . . . Indeed, these are all signs of the Lord to mark Padre Pio's holiness in a special way, but what we must not fail to do is to take his holy life as an example for ourselves. In this way, Padre Pio's teachings and life will really be of value to each of us. Look beyond the outward signs to his life hidden with Christ in God."[3]

Many *were* drawn to Pio initially because of his supernatural gifts. As in Padre Pio's case, when holiness accompanies the supernatural, the combination is especially attractive and has the effect of helping others to desire holiness and to grow in love of God and neighbor. That is why a saint like Pio is often surrounded by hundreds of followers or "spiritual children."

In order to grow in holiness, Pio urged his followers to ask Jesus for it. In a September 8, 1916, letter, Pio wrote, "To ask Jesus to make us holy is neither presumption nor audacity because it is the same as desiring to love God greatly."[4]

Pio also urged people to follow whatever advice Scripture offered. He knew that God speaks to us through his word, calling each of us to live a life of holiness, and that studying, praying, and meditating on Scripture helps us to become holy. "Trust in this authority," said Pio, "and do not fear the raging tempest because the little ship of your spirit will never be submerged. Heaven and earth will pass away, but the word of God, assuring us that whoever obeys will sing victory, will never pass away."[5]

Consumed by love for God and for his neighbor, Padre Pio never stopped trying to help others attain holiness, although he never considered himself holy. As one biographer noted, "It is the hallmark of the genuine quality of his holiness that he accepted all [trials and sufferings in his life] in simplicity."[6]

Pause: Have you ever asked Jesus to make you holy? What do you think he would say to you?

PIO'S WORDS

Let us try to improve our characters and model them on Jesus.... We must purify ourselves, like gold in the melting pot, by humbling ourselves, and Jesus will come down to us.[7]

Knowing that we can reach any degree of holiness only by belonging to God, who is holiness, Padre Pio wrote,

Those who belong totally to God are never afflicted except when they offend him, and in this case their affliction moves on to a profound, tranquil, and calm humility and submission, after which they are lifted up by divine goodness through a sweet and perfect confidence. . . . The one who belongs only to God seeks nobody but God himself, and given that God is equally great in times of tribulation and prosperity, one lives calmly in the midst of adversity.

He who belongs only to God continually thinks of him in the midst of all the events of this life, always tries to become better in the eyes of God, and finds and admires God in all creatures, exclaiming with Augustine, "All creatures, O Lord, tell me to love you."

Therefore, always belong to God and be nothing except in him, desiring nothing but to please him, in accordance with his will and for him. What greater blessing could I desire and seek for you from God? And so . . . be tranquil in him, like a child in the arms of its mother.[8]

REFLECTION

Pio led many people to Christ and then encouraged them to live holy lives and to express that holiness—as well as their love of God—by loving their neighbor. But is it possible for ordinary Christians like us to be holy and to love God as he desires? Jesus said, "Be perfect, therefore, as your heavenly Father is perfect" (Matthew 5:48). If loving God and attaining personal holiness were not possible, would Christ have told us to be "perfect," to be holy? On our own, of course, we can never attain any of the virtues, but we can do so by asking God to fulfill his will in us, to make us loving and holy. We can confidently place our trust in God by making St. Paul's words our own: "I can do all things through him who strengthens me" (Philippians 4:13).

Once we begin to follow the path of holiness and love, we can, like Padre Pio, best exercise that holiness and love by helping others, by practicing what Christian tradition calls the corporal and spiritual works of mercy. The corporal works are feeding the hungry, giving drink to the thirsty, clothing the naked, sheltering the traveler, comforting the prisoner, visiting the sick, and burying the dead. The spiritual works are teaching the ignorant, praying for the living and the dead, correcting sinners, counseling those in doubt, consoling the sorrowful, bearing wrongs patiently, and forgiving wrongs willingly.

Padre Pio's works of mercy manifested his love and holiness: through hours spent in the confessional listening to, admonishing, and counseling sinners; through the hundreds of letters he wrote; through each Mass he celebrated; through casual, everyday conversations; and through his constant humble acceptance of his physical, emotional, and spiritual sufferings. Following Pio's example, we too can practice holiness and love, and in doing so, ultimately reap the reward Jesus promises to all who do their best to help those in need: "Truly I tell you, just as you did it to one of the least of these who are members of my family, you did it to me" (Matthew 25:40).

❧ Imagine Jesus telling you that you have only six months to live. With your imminent death in mind, does your level of holiness suit you? Reflect on ways you could exercise your holiness and love of God by showing more love to others. Perhaps you could send a card or visit an elderly or sick person. Or, you might want to call someone you know who has recently experienced divorce or the death of a loved one. Spend the majority of the phone time listening to them. Make a list of other actions you could take to show the love of Christ to others.

❧ Create an epitaph for yourself that says what you would like others to say about you after you die. When you feel tempted to practice *un*holiness, recall your epitaph and ask the Holy Spirit to keep you pure—and purely for God.

❧ Think of ways to practice the corporal and spiritual works of mercy daily. For example, do you sometimes find it next to impossible to "bear wrongs patiently" or to "forgive wrongs willingly," especially when offended by someone close to you, perhaps someone in your own family? The next time someone offends you, ask the Holy Spirit to help you refrain from saying or doing anything that might be vengeful.

GOD'S WORD

Zechariah was filled with the Holy Spirit and spoke this prophecy: "Blessed be the Lord God of Israel, for he has looked favorably on his people and redeemed them. He has raised up a mighty savior for us in the house of his servant David, as he spoke through the mouth of his holy prophets from of old, that we would be saved from our enemies and from the hand of all who hate us. Thus he has shown the mercy promised to our ancestors, and has remembered his holy covenant, the oath that he swore to our ancestor Abraham, to grant us that we, being rescued from the hands of our enemies, might serve him without fear, in holiness and righteousness before him all our days." (Luke 1:67-75)

Closing Prayer: Knowing that we can lead holy lives only by clinging to Jesus, let us pray with Charlotte Elliot, who penned the old gospel hymn "Just as I Am":

Just as I am, without one plea,
    but that thy blood was shed for me,
And that thou bidd'st me come to thee,
O Lamb of God, I come! I come!
Just as I am and waiting not
    to rid my soul of one dark blot.
To thee, whose blood can cleanse each spot,
O Lamb of God, I come! I come! . . .
Just as I am, thou wilt receive,
Wilt welcome, pardon, cleanse, relieve,
Because thy promise I believe,
O Lamb of God, I come! I come![9]

1. Padre Pio, *Letters,* vol. 2, 3rd ed., ed. Gerardo Di Flumeri (San Giovanni Rotondo, Italy: Our Lady of Grace Capuchin Friary, 2002), p. 562.

2. Francis Kalvelage, ed., *Padre Pio: The Wonder Worker* (New Bedford, MA: Franciscan Friars of the Immaculate, n.d.), p. ix.

3. Alessio Parente, *Padre Pio Our Good Samaritan* (San Giovanni Rotondo, Italy: Our Lady of Grace Capuchin Friary, 1990), p. 190.

4. Padre Pio, *Letters,* vol. 3, 2nd ed., ed. Gerardo Di Flumeri (San Giovanni Rotondo, Italy: Our Lady of Grace Capuchin Friary, 2001), p. 253.

5. Pio, *Letters,* vol. 3, p. 253.

6. Malachy Carroll, *Padre Pio* (Dublin, Ireland: Cahill and Co. Limited, 1961), p. 23.

7. Nello Castello, *Padre Pio Teaches Us* (Bari, Italy: Favia Printers, 1981), pp. 27–28.

8. Pio, *Letters,* vol. 3, pp. 526–27.

9. Charlotte Elliot, "Just As I Am," in *Religious Favorites* (San Diego: Kjos West, 1978), p. 68.

Holy Angels Smile at Us

Theme: Padre Pio had an abiding awareness of angels and a remarkable relationship with his own guardian angel. He encouraged people to love the angels, to speak often to their own guardian angels, and to express their devotion to them. When asked if the angels smile at us, Padre Pio replied, "Of course."[1]

Opening Prayer: Lord, in your love and mercy you have assigned an angel to guard and guide me every moment of my life. Only you know how often and from what danger my guardian angel has protected me. Thank you, Lord, and bless this good angel of mine. Amen.

ABOUT PIO

As so many have done before us, we can find strength and courage in the psalmist's words, "The angel of the LORD encamps around those who fear him, and delivers them" (Psalm 34:7). Throughout Scripture, we find stories about God's angels rescuing people from danger. Angels also act as messengers of God. For example, the angel Gabriel delivered the news to Mary of Jesus' impending, miraculous birth.

Padre Pio's guardian angel rescued him countless times from

11/24/12 ← *1 00 yrs, + 19 days ago from today*

the assaults of the devil and other evil spirits. On November 5, 1912, Padre Pio wrote to his friend Fr. Agostino Daniele,

> I cannot tell you the way these scoundrels beat me. Sometimes I feel I am about to die. On Saturday it seemed to me that they intended to put an end to me. . . . I turned to my guardian angel and . . . there he was, hovering close to me, singing hymns to the divine Majesty in his angelic voice."[2]

Pio's guardian angel also acted as a messenger. According to biographer Fr. Stefano Manelli,

> Padre Pio lived in intimate contact with his guardian angel. . . . He used to keep Padre Pio up at night to chant God's praises with him . . . This angel thus became his helpmate and would carry messages from him to souls far away, bringing them comfort and blessings.
>
> One time Padre Pio wrote this about his angel, "Oh, the poor dear. He is too good. Does this not make me see my grave obligation of gratitude?"
>
> Padre Pio counseled many of his spiritual children to . . . entrust tasks to [their own angels], to have their angels go to Jesus and the Madonna, to this or that person. In his striking way of speaking, [Pio] encouraged souls to get their guardian angels to "fly" so as not to let "their wings rust."[3]

Pio's friend Fr. Alessio Parente wrote,

Being at Padre Pio's side for almost six years, I clearly understood that people sent their guardian angels to him when they wished to receive some message or to be remembered in his prayers. In fact, passing through the crowd with him as I did every day, I often heard it said, "Padre Pio, as I will not be able to come to see you again, what should I do if I need your prayers?" And Padre Pio would reply, "If you cannot come to me, send me your guardian angel. He can take a message from you to me, and I will assist you as much as I can."[4]

Not only did Pio want everyone to send messages to him through their guardian angels, he depended on his angel to help others whenever he asked the angel to do so. On July 28, 1913, Pio wrote this to his superior, Fr. Benedetto Nardella: "On the twentieth of this month I offered the holy Sacrifice for you. My good guardian angel knows this, and I have entrusted him many times with the delicate task of coming to you to console you."[5] With the childlike faith that Jesus encourages us to have (see Luke 18:17), Fr. Alessio continued to send messages to Pio via his own guardian angel, even after Pio had died. Today, when we need Pio to intercede for us with Jesus, we too can send our guardian angel to Pio with our messages.

Pause: Reflect on Pio's confidence in the angels and especially in his own guardian angel. Are you confident in the protection and care of your own guardian angel?

PIO'S WORDS

How consoling it is to know that near us is a spirit who, from the cradle to the tomb, does not leave us even for an instant, not even when we dare to sin. And this heavenly spirit guides and protects us like a friend, a brother, a sister. But it is extremely consoling to know that this angel prays without ceasing for us and offers to God all our good actions, our thoughts, and our desires, if they are pure.

For pity's sake, don't forget this invisible companion, always present, always ready to listen to you, and even more ready to console you. . . . Always keep him present to your mind's eye. . . . Turn to him in times of supreme anxiety and you will experience his beneficial help.

Never say you are alone in sustaining the battle against your enemies. Never say you have nobody to whom you can open up and confide. You would do this heavenly messenger a grave wrong.[6]

As his closest companion, Pio's guardian angel woke him in the morning and praised the Lord with him:

Again at night when I close my eyes, the veil is lifted,

and I see paradise open up before me; and gladdened by this vision I sleep with a smile of sweet beatitude on my lips and a perfectly tranquil countenance, waiting for the little companion of my childhood to come to waken me, so that we may sing together the morning praises to the Beloved of our hearts.[7]

Pio's angel also helped him translate foreign languages when foreign pilgrims confessed to him or wrote to him:

And while the mission of our guardian angels is a great one, my own angel's mission is certainly greater, since he has the additional task of teaching me other languages.[8]

In November of 1912, Pio told his superior how his guardian angel reassured him when he thought that the angel had ignored his request for help:

[The angel] said to me, "I am always close to you, my beloved young man. I am always hovering around you with the affection aroused by your gratitude to Jesus, the Beloved of your heart. This affection of mine will never end, not even when you die. I know that your generous heart beats all the time for the One we both love; you would cross every mountain and every desert in search of him, to see him again, to embrace him again in these extreme moments . . . but do not grow weary. . . . Jesus' supreme delight is to have you with him."[9]

REFLECTION

Pio knew that each holy angel represents to us a finite but exquisite part of God's infinite greatness and perfection. In some of the angels, we can see God's power. In others, we can see God's love and strength. Every angel reflects to us God's beauty and mercy. The angels continually adore, praise, and glorify our heavenly Father and yearn for us to join them. When we do so, we share in the divine life of the eternal Trinity with them.

The church encourages us to believe in our guardian angels and to trust them to act as God's agents to help us in times of need. We can follow Padre Pio's example of frequent, loving communication with his beloved angel. As we unite ourselves with the angels, we can praise God and bring others to him.

 When loneliness haunts you and makes you feel as if you have no one to confide in or to ask for help, remember that near you awaits a holy and constant companion assigned to you by God.

❧ Have you relegated guardian angels to the category of "comforting myths to reassure children"? Padre Pio said to turn to and have confidence in your own guardian angel and you will "experience his beneficial help." Through your own real experiences of your angel, you can learn to trust him or her always as a God-given companion. Jesus said, "Unless you change and become like children, you will never enter the kingdom of heaven" (Matthew 18:3). Ask Jesus to help you to become more "childlike" in order to accept the constant presence and help of your good angel. Resolve to acknowledge, love, and ask for the assistance of your angel more and more each day.

🕊 Are there areas of sin in your life that you find hard to share with your holy angel, let alone with God? Focus on a specific area that you find difficult to acknowledge or confess. Ask your guardian angel for help. Pray, through your angel's intercession, for the grace to embrace God's love for you. Ask for the grace to be more and more open to your angel and, above all, to God.

🕊 Allow Pio's image of your guardian angel as devoted friend, protector, confidante, and consoler to fill your imagination. Spend time meditating on this image, and then ask yourself these questions:

- How do I feel in the presence of this mighty friend assigned to me by God?

- What do I want to say to my good angel, and what might he or she reply to me?

🕊 Do you or someone you know have an urgent need or problem that you don't know how to address? Ask your guardian angel to take this need to Padre Pio. Pio will take your concern to Jesus. Have expectant faith that an answer will come.

GOD'S WORD

And the Spirit immediately drove [Jesus] out into the wilderness. He was in the wilderness forty days, tempted by Satan; and he was with the wild beasts; and the angels waited on him. (Mark 1:12-13)

Peter, bound with two chains, was sleeping between two soldiers, while guards in front of the door were keeping watch over the prison. Suddenly an angel of the Lord appeared and a light shone in the cell. He tapped Peter on the side and woke him, saying, "Get up quickly." And the chains fell off his wrists. The angel said to him, "Fasten your belt and put on your sandals." He did so. Then he said to him, "Wrap your cloak around you and follow me."

Peter went out and followed him; he did not realize that what was happening with the angel's help was real; he thought he was seeing a vision. After they had passed the first and the second guard, they came before the iron gate leading into the city. It opened for them of its own accord, and they went outside and walked along a lane, when suddenly the angel left him. (Acts 12:6-10)

And all the angels stood around the throne and around the elders and the four living creatures, and they fell on their

> faces before the throne and worshiped God, singing,
> "Amen! Blessing and glory and wisdom
> and thanksgiving and honor
> and power and might
> be to our God forever and ever! Amen."
> (Revelation 7:11-12)

Closing Prayer: Angel of God, my guardian dear, to whom God's love commits me here. Ever this day, be at my side, to light and guard, rule and guide. Amen. [Traditional prayer to a guardian angel]

1. Nello Castello, *Padre Pio Teaches Us* (Bari, Italy: Favia Printers, 1981), p. 17.

2. Padre Pio, *Letters*, vol. 1, 2nd ed., ed. Gerardo Di Flumeri (San Giovanni Rotondo, Italy: Our Lady of Grace Capuchin Friary, 1984), p. 351.

3. Stefano Manelli, *Padre Pio of Pietrelcina* (New Bedford, MA: Franciscans of the Immaculate, 1999), p. 52.

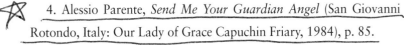

4. Alessio Parente, *Send Me Your Guardian Angel* (San Giovanni Rotondo, Italy: Our Lady of Grace Capuchin Friary, 1984), p. 85.

5. Pio, *Letters*, vol. 1, p. 443.

6. Padre Pio, *Letters*, vol. 3, 2nd ed., ed. Gerardo Di Flumeri (San Giovanni Rotondo, Italy: Our Lady of Grace Capuchin Friary, 2001), p. 85.

7. Pio, *Letters,* vol. 1, p. 347.

8. Pio, *Letters,* vol. 1, p. 343.

9. Pio, *Letters,* vol. 1, pp. 351–52.

Humility and Simplicity

Theme: Following Christ's example, Padre Pio lived a humble and simple life and stressed the importance of humility and simplicity as a path to the heart of God.

Opening Prayer: Here I am, Lord, your servant, nothing more. "Let it be with me according to your word" (Luke 1:38).

ABOUT PIO

As a monk living in a community, Padre Pio's daily routine reflected humility and simplicity. Throughout his long life at the monastery, he would not permit his will and judgment to take precedence over those of his fellow monks. Despite his many supernatural gifts, he refused to attribute importance of any kind to himself and never flaunted these gifts, knowing full well that God had given them to him.

Pio maintained an attitude of humility even in the face of intense media coverage. Author Maria Winowska, who knew Padre Pio, noted that in the 1950s, the media was trying hard to sensationalize Pio's spiritual gifts, including the stigmata. The resulting publicity threatened to cause the public to overlook who Pio really was: a holy priest. "Like St. John the Baptist," she wrote, "this humble monk asks but one thing: to 'diminish' so that Christ may 'increase' through him" [see John 3:30].[1]

Padre Pio was clearly uncomfortable with the admiration he received, and would shift the attention from himself to God when people spoke highly of him. One day, when Pio and his good friend John McCaffery were chatting, McCaffery mentioned that a new book had just been published in Ireland about Pio. Tears filled Pio's eyes, and he said, "You are all so mistaken. All of you. It is you who are good, not I." As McCaffery relates the story:

> "Well," I answered, "please leave us with our illusions because we are very fond of them." [Pio's] reply was serious and emphatic, "Listen. God made all things. His creation includes the stars and the humblest domestic utensil. I belong to the second category. . . . If I were to attribute to myself what belongs obviously and exclusively to God alone, there could be no other answer: I should have to be either mad or a thief."[2]

Pio's humility was accompanied by a simple lifestyle that was reflected in his humble childhood home in Pietrelcina, as well as in his austere cell at Our Lady of Grace Capuchin Friary. Like the other friars, he wore a rough Capuchin habit and ate sparingly. But his simplicity went beyond lifestyle. It was based on his single-hearted devotion to God and the peace this evoked in his heart. He wrote,

We should . . . not stop advancing in this beautiful virtue of simplicity. . . . But we will never advance even a single step in this virtue if we do not strive to live in a holy and immutable peace. Jesus' yoke is easy and his burden light, so we should not allow the enemy to creep into our hearts and rob us of this peace.

Peace is simplicity of heart, serenity of mind, tranquility of soul, the bond of love. Peace means order and harmony in our whole being; it means continual contentment springing from the knowledge of a good conscience; it is the holy joy of a heart in which God reigns. Peace is the way to perfection, indeed in peace is perfection found.[3]

To practice the virtue of simplicity in our lives, Pio recommended that we become "poor in spirit," as Christ had preached. Pio believed that to be poor in spirit, we have to remove from our hearts all attachments to worldly things. He believed that even a piece of old bread should not be wasted because "bread soup" could be made from it. He advised his followers to mend their clothes so that they could be worn as long as possible. If we do all we can to conserve and keep our lives simple, then we have more time and resources to spend loving and serving God and neighbor.

Pio's friend Malachy Carroll, who had assisted at many of Pio's Masses, wrote, "Humility is the bedrock of the whole spiritual edifice, and simplicity is its crown and glory. . . . It is this simplicity—as indefinable as the odor of a rose but as immediately perceptible—that impresses one most in Padre Pio."[4]

Pause: Reflect on the way humility helps you recognize God as the infinite parent and yourself as his finite child.

PIO'S WORDS

Self-love, self-esteem, and the false freedom of spirit are roots which one cannot easily remove from the heart. If you do good, praise and thank God; if you should fall into evil, humble yourself and blush with shame before God for your unfaithfulness, but without discouragement; ask pardon, make resolutions, and go back to the right road.

Always humble yourself lovingly before God and before man . . . never complain of offenses [done to you]. Excuse everyone. Do not be surprised at your weaknesses. Do not praise yourself for your virtues. Jesus has told us, "Apart from me you can do nothing" [John 15:5].[5]

Jesus likes to give himself to simple souls. We must make an effort to acquire this beautiful virtue of simplicity and to hold it in great esteem. Jesus said, "Truly I tell you, unless you change and become like children, you will never enter the kingdom of heaven" [Matthew 18:3]. But before Jesus taught us this by his words he had already put it into practice. He became a child and gave us the example of that simplicity he was to teach us later also by his words. Let us empty our hearts and keep far from us all human prudence. We must try to keep our thoughts pure, our ideas upright and honest, and our intentions holy.

We should also endeavor to have a will that seeks nothing but God and his glory. If we make every effort to advance in this beautiful virtue, he who teaches it will enrich us continually with new light and new heavenly favors.[6]

Let us look at ourselves in Jesus, as our mirror, in Jesus who led a hidden life. All his infinite majesty was hidden in the shadows and silence of that modest little workshop in Nazareth. So let us, too, make every effort to lead a completely interior life, hidden in God.[7]

REFLECTION

Padre Pio attributed holiness, gifts, and good works to the grace of God. He knew that all the credit for what he did belonged to Jesus, who worked through him. Like John the Baptist, he could say, "He must increase, but I must decrease" (John 3:30). Pio's humble attitude was accompanied by a simplicity that desired only that God be glorified. Pio simply wanted to do God's will in his life and thereby reflect God's glory, not his own.

✒ Pio recognized the inherent dignity of every person, no matter how poor, ill, or unpleasant they may be. Examine your conscience by recalling the times in the past week when you failed to recognize the dignity of others and thought more highly of yourself than them. Reflect on 1 Peter 5:5-6 at right, and then resolve to consider each person—regardless of any positive or negative feelings you might have for that person—as a child of God.

✒ Padre Pio left us many heartfelt exhortations, one of which is, "May you abandon yourself in the arms of the Lord with all the simplicity of a child."[8] Pray the following in harmony with slow, rhythmic breathing: "In your arms, Jesus, I find my peace."

✒ Do you sometimes take yourself too seriously? Do you cause yourself anxiety by thinking that the success of everything and everyone in your life depends on you? When that happens, sit or lie down on a comfortable surface such as a bed, carpet, or soft patch of grass. Close your eyes and imagine that the surface on which you are resting is the palm of God's hand. From the top of your head to the tips of your toes, gradually relax each part of your body, allowing God's "palm" to completely support you (see John 10:28-29 and Psalm 139:10).

✒ Light a candle either at church or at home. Gaze at the candle's flame and recall Jesus' words, "I am the light of the world"

(John 8:12). Silently or aloud, ask Jesus to be the light that leads you into a life of humility, simplicity, and peace.

GOD'S WORD

And all of you must clothe yourselves with humility in your dealings with one another, for 'God opposes the proud, but gives grace to the humble.' Humble yourselves therefore under the mighty hand of God, so that he may exalt you in due time. (1 Peter 5:5-6)

[Jesus said,] "Truly I tell you, unless you change and become like children, you will never enter the kingdom of heaven." (Matthew 18:3)

Closing Prayer: Jesus, so humble and meek, please make me more and more like you. Give me the peace of heart that comes from humility and simplicity.

1. Maria Winowska, *The True Face of Padre Pio* (London: Souvenir Press, 1955), p. 181.

2. John McCaffery, *The Friar of San Giovanni: Tales of Padre Pio* (London: Darton, Longman & Todd Ltd., 1983), pp. 66, 68.

3. Padre Pio, *Letters*, vol. 1, 2nd ed., ed. Gerardo Di Flumeri (San

Giovanni Rotondo, Italy: Our Lady of Grace Capuchin Friary, 1984), p. 678.

4. Malachy Carroll, *Padre Pio* (Dublin, Ireland: Cahill and Co. Limited, 1961), p. 69.

5. Alberto D'Apolito, *Padre Pio of Pietrelcina* (San Giovanni Rotondo, Italy: Our Lady of Grace Capuchin Friary, 1986), pp. 230–31.

6. Pio, *Letters*, vol. 1, pp. 677–78.

7. Padre Pio, *Letters*, vol. 2, 3rd ed., ed. Gerardo Di Flumeri (San Giovanni Rotondo, Italy: Our Lady of Grace Capuchin Friary, 2002), p. 140.

8. Nello Castello, *Padre Pio Teaches Us* (Bari, Italy: Favia Printers, 1981), p. 280.

Trusting Only in Jesus

Theme: Speaking to Jesus, Padre Pio said, "You wish to teach us that in you alone we must trust, even if heaven appears to us to be hardhearted."[1]

Opening Prayer: Lord Jesus, you tell us, "Come to me, all you that are weary and are carrying heavy burdens, and I will give you rest" (Matthew 11:28). Lord, I *am* weary from trying, on my own, to carry all my fears, worries, and burdens. Help me always to come to you, to place all my trust in you, and in you to find rest.

laundry

ABOUT PIO

Not only did Padre Pio advise everyone to put all their trust in Jesus, he also practiced what he preached. For example, Pio trusted Jesus to help him build a huge, modern hospital in San Giovanni. As testimony to Pio's trust and love, *Casa Sollievo della Sofferenza* (Home for the Relief of Suffering) is still one of the finest hospitals in Italy.

Pio wanted to build the hospital because, at the time, the lack of adequate medical care caused hundreds of infants in southern Italy to die from infectious diseases. Pio knew that he would need to trust Jesus for the necessary funding if the project were to become a reality.

The idea was ridiculed by many. Some called it "crazy" and said it would never succeed. How could a poor monk build a hospital on a rocky mountainside twenty-four hundred feet above sea level? Foggia, the nearest large town, lay twenty-five miles away. Without a railway system or modern highways leading to San Giovanni Rotondo, all materials would have to be created on site, including cement slabs and artificial marble. No water or electricity led to the proposed construction site. The greatest problem of all was financing. These obstacles caused many to doubt the feasibility of the project.

However, Padre Pio trusted God because Jesus said, "For mortals it is impossible, but for God all things are possible" (Matthew 19:26). Taking refuge in the Sacred Heart of Jesus, Pio entrusted the hospital project to divine providence. In January 1940, Pio decided, as an act of faith, to donate the only money he had to the project. He handed a small gold coin someone had just given him to two friends who were going to help him build the hospital.

World War II delayed the beginning of construction on the hospital, but on May 19, 1947, workers started clearing the land. With barely enough money to begin, Padre Pio and the hospital construction board promised themselves one thing: they would ask no one for financial help. They would trust God to inspire people to make donations to the project. Pio's unshakable faith had infected the members of the board, too.

Thousands of people responded with donations, even those who had little to give. A poor widow donated one banknote of Italian currency. Padre Pio knew that although this amount was very small, it was a great sacrifice for her, and he tried to make her keep the money. With tears in her eyes, she explained how she had saved the money for his hospital: "I don't buy matches, but instead light my fire from my neighbors' hearths. I put out my lamp very early and sometimes don't light it at all."[2] Like Jesus who accepted the poor widow's two small copper coins, Pio knew that this poor widow had trusted in God and given her all (see Mark 12:42-44). Her words touched Pio's heart, and he graciously accepted the donation.

On May 5, 1956, with a crowd of fifteen thousand people gathered for an outdoor Mass in front of the hospital, Padre Pio inaugurated the impressive new edifice. One biographer wrote, "Fervor, improvisation, holy foolhardiness, a will of iron, and an indestructible faith: these are the principal ingredients of an explosive mixture that can move mountains and bring about, at a dizzying pace, the construction of a monument to charity."[3] With Padre Pio at the helm of the project, the hospital became a reality that still serves the sick today.

Pause: When have you stepped out in faith like Pio and trusted Jesus to help you succeed in something that by human standards seemed impossible?

PIO'S WORDS

When I consider [Jesus' gentleness and graciousness], I am completely consoled. I cannot help abandoning myself to this tenderness, this happiness.[4]

Thanks to the favors with which God fills me incessantly, I have greatly improved as regards my trust in him. . . . I know from my own experience that the best way to avoid falling is to lean on the cross of Jesus with confidence in him alone, who for our salvation desired to be nailed to it.[5]

Let us always trust in God, and may our lively faith and the comfort of Christian hope assist us in this.[6]

The worst insult that one can offer to God is to doubt him.[7]

Let us call to mind that immense crowd of people of God in the desert, most of whom, for lack of trust in God, failed to set foot in the promised land. Even their leader, Moses, because he hesitated in striking the rock from which water was to come forth to quench the thirst of this people, was severely punished and did not enter the promised land [see Numbers 20:11-12].[8]

REFLECTION

What seemingly impossible project, mission, trial, or duty do you face today? You can turn to St. Pio and ask him to help you trust more and more in Jesus. When you cannot see the end of the road, when the path looks dark and frightening, your friend Pio will help you place everything in Jesus' hands. Christ will never forsake you in your need. As Pio said, "Lean on the cross of Jesus, with confidence in him alone, who for our salvation desired to be nailed to it."

Place a crucifix, no matter what size, in front of you. Sit in a relaxed posture, gazing at the crucifix and the figure of the crucified Christ. Imagine how much he had to trust the Father when he chose to suffer and die for us. Breathing deeply and slowly, concentrate on relaxing your body from the top of your head all the way to your toes. Continue to breathe deeply and slowly. As you do, repeat this Scripture passage again and again: "Trust in the LORD with all your heart, and do not rely on your own insight" (Proverbs 3:5). Do this until your mind is totally relaxed and you feel completely peaceful. When you are ready, still gazing at the crucifix, say to God, "I give you my heart and my all, and I place all my trust in you."

❧ On a sheet of paper or in your journal, list ways in which your life would improve if you placed all your trust in Jesus.

❧ Recall a recent time when you may have lost an opportunity to do a good work or act of charity because you failed to trust that Jesus would help you accomplish it. Examine how God may have been speaking to you during such times, encouraging you to step out in faith. Remember Peter on the water, responding to Jesus. If your trust wavers as Peter's did, reach out to Jesus and take his hand (see Matthew 14:29-31).

❧ Consider St. Paul's declaration and make it your own: "I can do all things through [Christ] who strengthens me" (Philippians 4:13). *NAB "I have the strength for everything through Him [Christ] who empowers me."*

❧ Meditate on the fact that Jesus laid down his life for you and will *never* desert you. Envision Jesus as a "bridge" over troubled waters, who will lay himself down to help you get across the turbulence.

GOD'S WORD

Surely God is my salvation; I will trust, and will not be afraid, for the LORD GOD is my strength and my might; he has become my salvation. (Isaiah 12:2)

Closing Prayer: Pray this shortened version of the prayer Padre Pio prayed every day for all those who asked for his intercession:

O my Jesus, you said, "Ask, and it will be given you; search, and you will find; knock, and the door will be opened for you" [Matthew 7:7]. Behold, I knock, I seek, and I ask for the grace of _____. *Sacred Heart of Jesus, I put all my trust in you.*

O my Jesus, you said, "Very truly, I tell you, if you ask anything of the Father in my name, he will give it to you" [John 16:23]. Behold, in your name I ask the Father for the grace of _____. *Sacred Heart of Jesus, I put all my trust in you.*

O Sacred Heart of Jesus, to whom one thing alone is impossible, namely, not to have compassion on the afflicted, have pity on us miserable sinners and grant us the grace which we ask of you through the sorrowful and immaculate heart of Mary, your and our tender mother. *Sacred Heart of Jesus, I put all my trust in you.*[9]

1. Maria Winowska, *The True Face of Padre Pio* (London: Souvenir Press, 1955), p. 172.

2. Dante Alimenti, *Padre Pio* (Bergamo, Italy: Editrice VELAR, 1984), p. 135.

3. Alimenti, *Padre Pio*, pp. 136, 138.

4. Padre Pio, *Letters*, vol. 1, 2nd ed., ed. Gerardo Di Flumeri (San Giovanni Rotondo, Italy: Our Lady of Grace Capuchin Friary, 1984), p. 357.

5. Pio, *Letters*, vol. 1, p. 519.

6. Pio, *Letters*, vol. 1, p. 666.

7. Winowska, *The True Face of Padre Pio*, title page.

8. Pio, *Letters*, vol. 1, p. 455.

9. Alessio Parente, *The Way of the Cross* (San Giovanni Rotondo, Italy: Our Lady of Grace Capuchin Friary, 1979), p. 48.

MEDITATION THIRTEEN

Mary

Theme: "May Mary be the star which shines on your path. . . . May she be like an anchor to which you must be more closely attached in time of trial."[1]

Opening Prayer: Lord Jesus, when you gave your mother to your apostle John at the foot of the cross, you gave her to all of us (see John 19:26-27). Help us to always love and honor her as our mother and yours.

ABOUT PIO

Padre Pio began experiencing visions of Mary, the mother of God, when he was only five years old. But his devotion to her was nurtured from birth. Each night, his parents would kneel down in their home with their children and recite the rosary.

Pio's love for the rosary only deepened as he studied for the priesthood and immersed himself in the Scripture passages that describe the mysteries of the rosary. As he studied the mysteries, he grew in love and appreciation for Mary and for her assent to God's request that she bear his son. According to Fr. Alessio Parente, who cared for Pio during his final years, Pio often said,

"Our Lady never refuses me a grace through the recitation of the rosary." Alessio explained,

Padre Pio's filial devotion and love for our blessed Lady knew no bounds. He was never seen without her rosary in his hand. He said, "Prayer is the key which opens up the heart of God," so it was through his prayer and his particular devotion to our Blessed Mother that he received, for others, so many graces.[2]

Pio's love for the rosary was demonstrated by the fact that he prayed it almost continually:

One day his superior asked him how many rosaries he recited daily. Padre Pio answered, "Well, I have to tell my superior the truth; I have recited thirty-four." For Pio, the rosary was a perpetual meditation on the profound mysteries of Calvary, on Jesus' plan of salvation, and on his sorrowful mother who was present.[3]

From childhood until death, Padre Pio's love for the mother of God continued to grow. By drawing ever closer to Mary, he felt ever closer to her divine Son. He knew that since God had chosen Mary as the vessel through which he gave us the Christ Child, we should trust God to use Mary to draw us closer to him.

Pause: Do you turn to Mary so that you can draw closer to Jesus?

PIO'S WORDS

I feel myself held fast and bound to the Son by means of this mother, without seeing the chains which bind me so tightly.[4]

The Immaculate Conception is the first step on the path to salvation. She spurts like a ray of light from the thought of God. . . . All grace passes through her hands.[5]

May the virgin of sorrows obtain for us the grace to penetrate always further into the mystery of the cross. May she obtain for us the love of the cross, of suffering, and of sorrows, and may she who was the first to live the Gospel in all its perfection, and in all its severity, gain for us the impulse to follow her immediately.[6]

How often have I confided to this mother the painful anxieties that troubled my heart? And how often has she consoled me? . . . In my greatest sufferings it seems to me that I no longer have a mother on this earth but a very compassionate one in heaven. . . . Poor dear Mother, how you love me.[7]

How far away is the hope of victory, viewed from this land of exile. How close and certain it is, on the other hand, when viewed from God's house, beneath the protection of this most holy mother.[8]

REFLECTION

Padre Pio did not hesitate to ask Mary to obtain for him the grace he needed to grow in his love for God. He trusted that the eternal life her divine Son now shared with her in heaven placed her in the perfect position from which to ask favors of God. Scripture, church tradition, and meditation on the mysteries of the rosary had shown Pio that God the Father chose Mary to be the vessel through which he brought our Savior into the world. And from that truth, Pio rightly deduced that Mary continues to be a vessel through which God gives his graces, mercy, and love to us. From her consent to God's conception of the Christ child in her womb, to her sharing in her divine Son's suffering during his crucifixion, to her eternal life now with him in heaven, Mary was—and is—always ready to help us. While on earth, Padre Pio never hesitated to go to Mary for help, and he always recommended that we too not shrink from seeking her aid.

🍃 Do you know someone who needs the unconditional, tender love of a mother? Share with them how Mary, the mother of

God, can give them the love they desire. Then offer to bring to Mary their petitions and needs.

&. Reflect on the image of the pregnant Mary as the tabernacle of the Lord, while meditating on Pio's words, "Purify my heart . . . purify my spirit . . . purify my body that it may become for him a living tabernacle."[9] How can you, like Mary, bear Christ in the world?

&. Select from "Pio's Words" a passage that you especially find meaningful. As you pray this passage over and over, let its meaning saturate your heart, mind, and soul.

&. Pio addressed Mary by many titles. Choose one or more and spend some time meditating on how Mary's life is reflected in that title. Which one most appeals to you?

Sorrowful Mother
Model of Purity and Sanctity
Most Perfect of Creatures
Mother of the Most High
Gentle Mother
Channel of Christ
Incomparable Masterpiece of the Creator
Tabernacle of the Most High

GOD'S WORD

In the sixth month the angel Gabriel was sent . . . to a virgin engaged to a man whose name was Joseph, of the house of David. The virgin's name was Mary. And he came to her and said, "Greetings, favored one! The Lord is with you. . . . Do not be afraid, Mary, for you have found favor with God. And now, you will conceive in your womb and bear a son, and you will name him Jesus. He will be great, and will be called the Son of the Most High, and the Lord God will give to him the throne of his ancestor David. He will reign over the house of Jacob forever, and of his kingdom there will be no end." Mary said to the angel, "How can this be, since I am a virgin?" The angel said to her, "The Holy Spirit will come upon you, and the power of the Most High will overshadow you; therefore the child to be born will be holy; he will be called Son of God." . . . Then Mary said, "Here am I, the servant of the Lord; let it be with me according to your word." (Luke 1:26-38)

Closing Prayer: "My most pure mother . . . in your goodness deign, I beseech you, to pour out on me at least a little of the grace that flowed into you with such infinite profusion from the heart of God. Strengthened and supported by this grace, may I succeed in better loving and serving almighty God, who filled your heart completely and who created the temple of your body from the moment of your Immaculate Conception. . . . Cleanse my mind that it may reach up to God and contemplate him and adore him in spirit and in truth. Purify my body that I, too, may be a tabernacle for him and be less unworthy of possessing him when he deigns to come to me in Holy Communion."[10]

1. Padre Pio, *Letters,* vol. 2, 3rd ed., ed. Gerardo Di Flumeri (San Giovanni Rotondo, Italy: Our Lady of Grace Capuchin Friary, 2002), p. 389.

2. Alessio Parente, *Send Me Your Guardian Angel* (San Giovanni Rotondo, Italy: Our Lady of Grace Capuchin Friary, 1984), p. 190.

3. Francesco Napolitano, *Padre Pio of Pietrelcina* (San Giovanni Rotondo, Italy: Edizioni "Voce di Padre Pio," 1979), pp. 222–23.

4. Padre Pio, *Letters,* vol. 1, 2nd ed., ed. Gerardo Di Flumeri (San Giovanni Rotondo, Italy: Our Lady of Grace Capuchin Friary, 1984), p. 402.

5. Maria Winowska, *The True Face of Padre Pio* (London: Souvenir Press, 1955), p. 181.

6. Alessio Parente, *Our Lady of Grace Prayer Book* (San Giovanni Rotondo, Italy: Our Lady of Grace Capuchin Friary, 1988), p. 189.

7. Pio, *Letters,* vol. 1, pp. 311–12.

8. Pio, *Letters,* vol. 1, p. 645.

9. Winowska, *The True Face of Padre Pio,* p. 182.

10. Padre Pio, *Meditation Prayer on Mary Immaculate* (Rockford, IL: Tan Books and Publishers, Inc., 1974), pp. 7–8.

Fear Not, Worry Not

Theme: "Have no fear . . . and don't even ask where the Lord is because he is within you," said Pio. "And in him and in his arms, no misfortune of any kind can befall you."[1] "All your worries . . . should be placed in total abandonment in the arms of the heavenly Father, as he takes supreme care that your soul, which is so dear to him, may not be subject to the power of the evil one."[2]

Opening Prayer: Forgive me for my fears and worries, Lord, for they reveal a lack of faith in you. Worrying accomplishes nothing good. Be my strength, Jesus, and fill me with your love that casts out fear (see 1 John 4:18).

ABOUT PIO

Padre Pio warned that fear itself is worse than the things we fear. As a remedy for fear and worry, Pio advised, "Pray, hope, and don't worry."[3] Throughout his lifetime, he had plenty of opportunities to put this advice into practice.

From his youth, Pio suffered from perennially frail health. Because of his poor health, he received private tutoring at home. When he was fifteen, he entered the Capuchin order. In the sheltered life of the monastery, however, his health failed to improve for lack of rest caused by almost daily attacks from evil spirits.

Throughout Padre Pio's life, along with visions of his guardian angel, Jesus, and Mary, Pio also had visions of evil spirits. Fear and worry about these visions could have overwhelmed Pio, but his faith in God overcame them. One author who knew him wrote,

> The higher Pio mounted up the scale of perfection, the more fiercely did evil attack him. One night he saw his bed surrounded by the most fearful monsters who shouted, "See, the saint is retiring." "Yes, in spite of you," answered Pio, and he was promptly seized, shaken, and beaten to the floor. The more he was tormented by evil, the greater grew his faith and his love for our Lord.
>
> Another time when Padre Pio was ill in bed, he saw a friar come into his room who looked like his confessor, Fr. Agostino. The apparition proceeded to advise him to give up his practice of penance because God did not approve of it. Pio, much astonished, ordered his visitor to call out, "Long live, Jesus." Now silent, the strange creature disappeared, leaving behind a strong smell of sulfur.[4]

Padre Pio also experienced apparitions of souls from purgatory, who visited him on a regular basis to ask him for his prayers. When the apparitions first began, they distressed him,

"Song" "For I am Crucified With Christ"

but he soon conquered his fear and anxiety over them. Fr. Alessio Parente, who cared for Pio in his later years, noted, "Bishop Costa had come from the diocese of Melfi, Italy, to visit Padre Pio, and while in conversation with him, the bishop asked if he had ever seen a soul from purgatory. Padre Pio answered, 'I have seen so many that they don't frighten me anymore.'"[5]

Pio could also have worried that the constant bleeding from his stigmata would lead to an early death. However, he seemed to adopt the attitude of St. Paul, who wrote, "Living is Christ and dying is gain. If I am to live in the flesh, that means fruitful labor for me; and I do not know which I prefer" (Philippians 1:21-22).

Through all his experiences, Pio learned the worthlessness of fear and worry. He knew that because he had forever abandoned himself into God's loving arms, God controlled everything in his life, and so there was no point in being fearful or anxious.

Pause: Why was Pio able to completely surrender to God? How can you become free from worry and fear?

PIO'S WORDS

Jesus, whom you call and believe you have lost, is totally yours. He is so closely united to you . . . you possess him. What do you fear then? Listen to God who says to Abraham and to you also, 'Do not be afraid, I am your shield" [Genesis 15:1]. What do you seek on earth if not God? Well then, I tell you . . . that you possess him. Be firm in your resolutions, stay in the boat in which Jesus has placed you, and let the storm come. . . . You will not perish. To you he appears to be sleeping, but at the opportune time he will awaken to restore your calm. Scripture tells us that at the sight of the storm our St. Peter was frightened, and trembling he exclaimed, "O Lord, save me!" And our Lord, taking him by the hand, said to him, "You of little faith, why did you doubt?" [Matthew 14:31]. Observe this holy apostle. He walks with dry feet on the water; the waves and winds do not submerge him, but the *fear* of the wind and waves discourages him. Fear is a greater evil than evil itself.

I also repeat to you with the divine Master, "Why are you afraid?" No, you are walking on the sea amidst the wind and waves, but be sure that you are with Jesus. What is there to fear? But if fear takes you by surprise, you, too, shout loudly, "Lord, save me!" He will stretch out his hand to you; and this hand is precisely that tenuous ray of trust in him which you feel in the depth of your soul. Squeeze his hand tightly and walk joyfully.[6]

Do not anticipate the problems of this life with apprehension, but rather with a perfect hope that God, to whom you belong, will free you from them accordingly.

bk. Abandonmnt, to Divine Providenc

He has defended you up to now. Simply hold on tightly to the hand of his divine providence and he will help you in all events, and when you are unable to walk, he will lead you, don't worry. Why should you fear when you belong to this God who strongly assures us, "We know that all things work together for good for those who love God" (Romans 8:28)? Don't think about tomorrow's events because the same heavenly Father who takes care of you today will do the same tomorrow and forever.[7]

REFLECTION

God will take care!

Padre Pio's freedom from fear and worry stemmed from his overriding faith in God's providence. Pio bolstered his faith, as well as that of others who sought his counsel, by truly believing what God says in Scripture: "We know that all things work together for good for those who love God, who are called according to his purpose" (Romans 8:28). In fact, this Scripture verse was one of his most often quoted passages in his four volumes of letters.

What can we learn from Padre Pio's faith? Although Pio endured emotional, physical, and spiritual suffering, he lived a life of faith and was able to keep his focus on his final destination: heaven. If Jesus took care of Pio, will he not also take care of you, as well as your entire family? All you must do is put your trust and hope in God.

❧ Consider your present situations at home, work, or school. What are your greatest worries and fears in each of those situations? Examine your conscience to see if a lack of trust in God's loving providence might be causing your fears and worries. Open up to Jesus, confessing your weaknesses, failures, worries, and fears. Then resolve, by his grace, to relinquish everything into his loving care. This will help you accept his will—not your own—in all situations.

❧ Find a place, indoors or outdoors, where you can maintain a prayerful quietness. Breathe slowly and deeply. Each time you inhale, say, "I place everything into your hands, Lord," and realize that you really *do* want to follow God's will in everything. Every time you slowly exhale, say, "Thy will be done," and relinquish to God every fear and worry that you have. Whenever anxiety or fear threaten to defeat you, repeat this breathing-meditating-relinquishing process and experience the deep relaxation and peace that God wants to give you.

❧ "Give and it will be given to you" (Luke 6:38). If you are worried or fearful yourself, make it a point to meet with one or two people you know who are also suffering from worry and fear. Through your compassionate presence, allow the Holy Spirit to use you to give them comfort, love, and assurance. In giving of yourself, you will find that God has eased your own fears and worries.

GOD'S WORD

[Jesus said,] "Therefore I tell you, do not worry about your life, what you will eat or what you will drink, or about your body, what you will wear. Is not life more than food, and the body more than clothing? Look at the birds of the air; they neither sow nor reap nor gather into barns, and yet your heavenly Father feeds them. Are you not of more value than they? And can any of you by worrying add a single hour to your span of life? . . . So do not worry about tomorrow, for tomorrow will bring worries of its own. Today's trouble is enough for today." (Matthew 6:25-34)

[Jesus said,] "Do not fear those who kill the body but cannot kill the soul; rather fear him who can destroy both soul and body in hell. Are not two sparrows sold for a penny? Yet not one of them will fall to the ground apart from your Father. And even the hairs of your head are all counted. So do not be afraid; you are of more value than many sparrows." (Matthew 10:28-31)

Closing Prayer: Lord God, forgive me for the times I have allowed myself to be controlled by fear and worry. Give me the grace to believe that you are my shepherd, and that no matter what dark valley I walk through, I will not be afraid, because you are with me.

1. Padre Pio, *Letters*, vol. 3, 2nd ed., ed. Gerardo Di Flumeri (San Giovanni Rotondo, Italy: Our Lady of Grace Capuchin Friary, 2001), p. 198.

2. Pio, *Letters*, vol. 3, p. 167.

3. Pio, *Letters*, vol. 3, p. 167.

4. Dorothy M. Gaudiose, *Padre Pio* (Westwood, NJ: Westwood Printing, n.d.), p. 6.

5. Alessio Parente, *The Holy Souls* (San Giovanni Rotondo, Italy: Our Lady of Grace Capuchin Friary, 1990), p. 35.

6. Pio, *Letters*, vol. 3, pp. 177–78.

7. Pio, *Letters*, vol. 3, p. 730.

MEDITATION FIFTEEN

Joy in the Lord

Theme: "Joy is born of happiness at possessing what we love. Now, from the moment in which the soul knows God, it is naturally led to love him. . . . By loving God, the soul is certain of possessing him. . . . Joy, then, is an offspring of love."[1]

Opening Prayer: Lord, fill me with your love so that I may radiate the joy of being your child. Then use me to share your love and joy with everyone I meet.

ABOUT PIO

As a devoted spiritual son of St. Francis of Assisi, Padre Pio imitated his joyful spirit. The joy of both saints sprang from their intense love of God and from remaining at all times in his presence as they experienced the words of the psalmist: "In your presence there is fullness of joy" (Psalm 16:11).

Like St. Francis, Padre Pio also embraced with joy and gratitude a life of poverty and asceticism for the love of Christ. What G. K. Chesterton said about St. Francis can also be said about Pio: "The whole point about St. Francis of Assisi is that he certainly was ascetical, and he certainly was not gloomy. . . . He devoured fasting as a man devours food. He plunged after poverty as men have dug madly for gold."[2] Pio found joy in bearing these and other crosses: "I have no wish whatsoever to have my cross lightened, for it is a joy for me to suffer with Jesus. When I contemplate the cross on the shoulders of Jesus, I feel myself strengthened and I exult with holy joy."[3]

Padre Pio's joy of the Lord was often expressed as tears. He told onlookers that these tears were tears of joy in gratitude to the Lord for his countless blessings. Sometimes following the end of Mass, while kneeling and giving thanks to God, Padre Pio would weep, but not out of sadness. "When paradise is poured into a heart, this afflicted, exiled, weak, and mortal heart cannot bear it without weeping," he explained. "I repeat that it was the joy that filled my heart which caused me to weep for so long."[4] On April 18, 1912, describing his experiences during his thanksgiving directly after Mass, Pio wrote,

There were things which cannot be translated into human language without losing their deep and heavenly meaning. The heart of Jesus and my own—allow me to use the expression—were fused. No longer were two hearts beating but only one. My own heart had disappeared, as a drop of water is lost in the ocean. Jesus was its paradise, its King. My joy was so intense and deep that I could bear no more, and tears of happiness poured down my cheeks.[5]

In spite of his constant suffering and the seriousness of his mission, when Pio relaxed in his cell or in the monastery garden with friends and fellow friars, he displayed an infectious sense of humor. The biographer Dorothy Gaudiose, who spent several years in San Giovanni Rotondo, wrote,

All those who knew Padre Pio heard him tell funny stories; indeed he must have had a whole anthology of them in his head. His answers were full of humor and he liked a joke. He was in the monastery garden one evening listening to the complaints of some of his spiritual sons. Suddenly he smiled and said, "None of you are happy, only we monks are happy, do you know why?" Then he made the sign of the cross and said: "We have no debts, we have no credit, we have no wives, nor any children and so be it!"

Once when an internationally known political figure turned up at San Giovanni Rotondo accompanied by a police motorcycle escort, he received this welcome from Pio: "Well, well, how the world has changed since I was young! In those days the police were to be found at the heels of thieves and robbers. Now they go before them on motorcycles to clear the way!"[6]

Padre Pio had a "frank, innocent smile that stemmed from a pure heart," according to biographer Francesco Napolitano. Pio's humor and natural mannerisms made his supernatural gifts all the more incredible: "Between a smile and a joke he hid his secret [his mysticism], so that many people who lived near him never suspected anything; some never even understood his goodness and his heroic virtues. . . . He was always between two lives, smiling and exchanging words with the beings of two worlds.[7]

Pause: How much joy do you experience in your day-to-day life?

PIO'S WORDS

Preserve a spirit of holy joyfulness, which, being modestly spread throughout your actions and words, brings consolation to people, the children of God, so that they may glorify God for it. . . . Be tranquil in everything. Never permit your soul to become sad—to live with a sad scrupulous spirit—because Jesus is the Spirit of sweetness and is completely lovable toward those who want to love him.[8]

Now and again, a most feeble light penetrates from above, just enough to reassure my poor soul that all is being directed by divine providence, and that, through joy and tears, the heavenly Father is leading me by inscrutable secret ways to the end he has in view. This is nothing else than the perfection of my soul and its union with God.[9]

When you fail in some way due to infirmity, you should not be surprised at all, but while detesting on the one hand the offence to God, on the other you must conceive a certain joyful humility at the sight and knowledge of your miseries.[10]

Nothing can dry up and actually does dry up the milk and honey of charity like regrets, affliction, and melancholy. Live, then, in holy joy among people. Give them spiritual comfort, kindly and graciously, so that they may seek it gladly.[11]

REFLECTION

As did his spiritual father St. Francis of Assisi, Padre Pio believed a Christian should exhibit joy rather than sadness, because one of the gifts of the Holy Spirit is joy (see Galatians 5:22). "Avoid appearing gloomy, sad, and clouded, like the hypocrites," said St. Francis, "but let [yourself] ever be found joyous in the Lord."[12] In spite of his almost constant sufferings, Padre Pio followed Francis' advice and tried to display the joy God had placed within his heart.

How can we be filled with the joy of the Lord? Padre Pio advised us to draw close to God, the source of all joy. As we remain in God's presence and love, we will experience a joy that does not depend on the current circumstances of our lives but on the gratitude we feel as children of our heavenly Father.

❧ Think about the people in your life. Who complains about their problems, whether physical, emotional, or spiritual? Do these people project a spirit of joy and peace? Think next about the people in your life who seldom complain. Do these people project a spirit of joy and peace? Does complaining ever produce anything positive? Make a resolution that the next time you are tempted to complain, you will say something positive instead and express gratitude to the Lord. Over the next few weeks, practice this spiritual exercise. Expect joy and peace to increase within you.

❧ Do you have a particular scene from Scripture that speaks of joy to you? Spend a few minutes meditating on its meaning for you. Reflect on the joy and gratitude in the scene of the resurrection in John 20:14-17. Or meditate on the joyful scene in which the resurrected Christ appeared to Thomas (see John 20:26-29).

❧ Commit to memory this verse from Nehemiah 8:10: "The joy of the LORD is [my] strength." Repeat this phrase over and over during the next few days whenever you have a few moments of inactivity or whenever you have a particular need for God's strength and encouragement.

GOD'S WORD

[Jesus said,] "So you have pain now; but I will see you again, and your hearts will rejoice, and no one will take your joy from you." (John 16:22)

Listen to me, you that pursue righteousness, you that seek the LORD. . . . For the LORD will comfort Zion; he will comfort all her waste places, and will make her wilderness like Eden, her desert like the garden of the LORD; joy and gladness will be found in her, thanksgiving and the voice of song. (Isaiah 51:1-3)

The fruit of the Spirit is love, joy, peace. . . .
(Galatians 5:22)

My brothers and sisters, whenever you face trials of any kind, consider it nothing but joy, because you know that the testing of your faith produces endurance; and let endurance have its full effect, so that you may be mature and complete, lacking in nothing. (James 1:2-4)

Closing Prayer: Lord Jesus, the thought of you and the knowledge of your presence fills me with joy. Purify my heart and mind so that your Holy Spirit may dwell within me and always lead me in the paths of joy and peace.

1. Padre Pio, *Letters*, vol. 2, 3rd ed., ed. Gerardo Di Flumeri (San Giovanni Rotondo, Italy: Our Lady of Grace Capuchin Friary, 2002), p. 214.

2. G. K. Chesterton, "The Ungloomy Ascetic," in *The Francis Book*, ed. Roy Gasnick (New York: Macmillan Publishing Co., Inc., 1980), p. 58.

3. Alessio Parente, *Our Lady of Grace Prayer Book* (San Giovanni Rotondo, Italy: Our Lady of Grace Capuchin Friary, 1988), p. 185.

4. Padre Pio, *Letters*, vol. 1, 2nd ed., ed. Gerardo Di Flumeri (San Giovanni Rotondo, Italy: Our Lady of Grace Capuchin Friary, 1984), p. 308.

5. Pio, *Letters*, vol. 1, p. 308.

6. Dorothy M. Gaudiose, *Padre Pio* (Westwood, NJ: Westwood Printing, n.d.), pp. 13–14.

7. Francesco Napolitano, *Padre Pio of Pietrelcina* (San Giovanni Rotondo, Italy: Edizioni "Voce di Padre Pio," 1979), p. 196–97, pp. 210–11.

8. Padre Pio, *Letters*, vol. 3, 2nd ed., ed. Gerardo Di Flumeri (San Giovanni Rotondo, Italy: Our Lady of Grace Capuchin Friary, 2001), p. 779.

9. Pio, *Letters*, vol. 1, p. 665.

10. Pio, *Letters*, vol. 3, p. 675.

11. Pio, *Letters*, vol. 1, p. 1087.

12. Knowles, Leo, *Catholic Book of Quotations* (Huntington, IN: Our Sunday Visitor Publishing Division, Our Sunday Visitor, Inc., 2004), p. 203.

Appendix: Becoming St. Pio's Spiritual Child

In August 1968, the month before Padre Pio died, he said, "I belong completely to everyone. Everyone can say, 'Padre Pio is mine.' I love my brothers and sisters in exile so much. I love my spiritual children as much as my own soul and even more. . . . I can forget myself, but not my spiritual children; indeed I assure you that when the Lord calls me I will tell him, 'Lord, I will remain by the door of paradise and come in when I have seen the last of my children enter'" (Dante Alimenti, *Padre Pio* [Bergamo, Italy: Editrice VELAR, 1984], pp. 168–70).

If you would like to become one of Pio's spiritual children, simply contact one of the following:

Convent of the Capuchin Minor Friars
Our Lady of Grace Sanctuary
71013 San Giovanni Rotondo, Italy
E-mail: thevoice@vocedipadrepio.com
Web site: www.vocedipadrepio.com

National Centre for Padre Pio, Inc.
2213 Old Route 100
Barto, PA 19504
telephone: 610-845-3000
fax: 610-845-2666
Web site: www.padrepio.org
E-mail: info@padrepio.org

Acknowledgments

Selections from the following books and articles are reprinted with permission of Our Lady of Grace Capuchin Friary, San Giovanni Rotondo, Italy:

Abresch, Frederico. *The Voice of Padre Pio*, copyright © 1954.

Capuchin Friars Minor. *The Charisms of Padre Pio: Calendar 2006*, copyright © 2005.

D'Apolito, Alberto. *Padre Pio of Pietrelcina: Memories, Experiences, Testimonials*, copyright © 1986.

Di Flumeri, Gerardo, OFM Cap. *Letters*, Vol. 1, 2nd ed., copyright © 1984; *Letters*, Vol. 2, 3rd ed., copyright © 2002; *Letters*, Vol. 3, 3rd ed., copyright © 2001; *The Mystery of the Cross in Padre Pio of Pietrelcina*, copyright © 1977.

Parente, Alessio, OFM Cap. *Have a Good Day*, copyright © 1990; *The Holy Souls: "Viva Padre Pio,"* copyright © 1990; *Our Lady of Grace Prayer Book*, copyright © 1988; *Padre Pio, Our Good Samaritan*, copyright © 1990; *Padre*

Pio's Prayer Life, English edition, copyright © 1994; *Send Me Your Guardian Angel*, copyright © 1984; *The Way of the Cross*, copyright © 1979.

The following books and articles are reprinted with permission of The Voice of Padre Pio, San Giovanni Rotondo, Italy, www.vocedipadrepio.com:

Colacelli, Francesco D. "An Affinity That Continues." In *The Voice of Padre Pio*, vol. 35, ed. Capuchin Friars, Nov.–Dec., 2005, p. 3.

Gravina, Luigi. "The Vigil of Saint Pio." In *The Voice of Padre Pio*, vol. 35, ed. Capuchin Friars, Nov.–Dec., 2005, p. 20.

Lilley, Stella Maris. *On the Road with Padre Pio*, Edizoni Padre Pio da Pietrelcina.

Napolitano, Francesco. *Padre Pio of Pietrelcina: Brief Biography*, copyright © 1979.

Preziuso, Gennaro. "The Parents of Padre Pio." In *The Voice of Padre Pio*, vol. 35, ed. Capuchin Friars, Nov.–Dec., 2005, pp. 9–12.

Titles in the Companions for the Journey Series

Praying with Anthony of Padua
Praying with Benedict
Praying with C. S. Lewis
Praying with Catherine McAuley
Praying with Catherine of Siena
Praying with Clare of Assisi
Praying with Dominic
Praying with Dorothy Day
Praying with Elizabeth Seton
Praying with Francis of Assisi
Praying with Francis de Sales
Praying with Frédéric Ozanam
Praying with Hildegard of Bingen
Praying with Ignatius of Loyola
Praying with John Cardinal Newman
Praying with John of the Cross
Praying with Pope John Paul II
Praying with Teresa of Ávila
Praying with Thérèse of Lisieux
Praying with Thomas Aquinas
Praying with Vincent de Paul

Order from
The Word Among Us Press
9639 Dr. Perry Rd., #126
Ijamsville, MD, 21754
1-800-775-9673
www.wordamongus.org

Also in the Companions for the Journey Series

Praying with Ignatius of Loyola
Jacqueline Syrup Bergan and Marie Schwan, CSJ
160 pages, 5¼ x 8, softcover
Item# BSMDE3

Praying with Thérèse of Lisieux
Joseph F. Schmidt, FSC
160 pages, 5¼ x 8, softcover
Item# BSMUE3

Praying with Pope John Paul II
Jo Garcia-Cobb and Keith E. Cobb
176 pages, 5¼ x 8, softcover
Item# BSM1E5

Praying with Francis of Assisi
Joseph M. Stoutzenberger
and John D. Bohrer
5¼ x 8, softcover, 144 pages
Item# BSMOE3

To order call 1-800-775-9673 or order online at www.wordamongus.org